More Praise for
Instructional Design on a Shoestring

"This veritable playbook for effective instructional design—even with limited resources—will get you off the sidelines and onto the field. Leverage this easy-to-follow guide to help you deliver optimal solutions and results for your learners, your leaders, and your organization."

—**Lorri Freifeld,** Editor and Publisher, *Training* Magazine

"Brian Washburn's *Instructional Design on a Shoestring* presents a radically simplified approach to the often-complex job of designing and developing training. He provides tools, resources, and processes to increase your efficiency and cost effectiveness, giving you the time for more creativity and innovation in your learning design. A must-have guide for any learning designer!"

—**Brandon Carson,** Global Head of L&D, Starbucks

"This will easily become the go-to resource for anyone who wants to design learning that creates effective results. Brian Washburn is 'ruthless' at helping readers learn how to ask the right questions to get to the right solutions, no matter the length of the shoestring."

—**Kassy LaBorie,** Speaker, Consultant, and Author of *Interact and Engage! 75+ Activities for Virtual Training, Meetings, and Webinars*

"*Instructional Design on a Shoestring* is a terrific text for the e-learning or instructional designer faced with an all-too-common problem—not having access to all the resources available to design training. This book will be useful for my training and development students and to professionals who are asked to build training with few resources. This book would have helped me immensely when I was starting my career, and I believe it will help you too."

—**Sy Islam,** Vice President of Consulting, Talent Metrics

"This is an insightful guide to maximizing your instructional design project's brilliance even within budget constraints. The author expertly weaves together strategies, tools, services, and resources that are readily implementable."

—**Kate Udalova,** Founder, 7taps Microlearning

On a
Shoestring
Series

Instructional
Design
on a Shoestring

Brian Washburn

atd
PRESS
Alexandria, VA

© 2024 ASTD DBA the Association for Talent Development (ATD)
All rights reserved. Printed in the United States of America.

27 26 25 24   1 2 3 4 5

No part of this publication may be reproduced, distributed, or transmitted in any form or by any means, including photocopying, recording, information storage and retrieval systems, or other electronic or mechanical methods, without the prior written permission of the publisher, except in the case of brief quotations embodied in critical reviews and certain other noncommercial uses permitted by copyright law. For permission requests, please go to copyright.com, or contact Copyright Clearance Center (CCC), 222 Rosewood Drive, Danvers, MA 01923 (telephone: 978.750.8400; fax: 978.646.8600).

ATD Press is an internationally renowned source of insightful and practical information on talent development, training, and professional development.

ATD Press
1640 King Street
Alexandria, VA 22314 USA

Ordering information: Books published by ATD Press can be purchased by visiting ATD's website at td.org/books or by calling 800.628.2783 or 703.683.8100.

Library of Congress Control Number: 2023942650

ISBN-10: 1-95394-695-X
ISBN-13: 978-1-953946-95-9
e-ISBN: 978-1-95715-710-8

ATD Press Editorial Staff
Director: Sarah Halgas
Manager: Melissa Jones
Content Manager, Learning and Development: Jes Thompson
Developmental Editor: Jack Harlow
Production Editor: Katy Wiley Stewts
Text and Cover Designer: Shirley E.M. Raybuck
Text Layout: PerfecType

Printed by BR Printers, San Jose, CA

To Tim, Heather, Lauren, Rachel, Lindsay, Erin, (not) Jess, and Hannah
You are the dream team that truly makes miracles happen.

To Beth
Let's venture beyond—whether it's on a shoestring or not.

Contents

About the On a Shoestring Series ix

Introduction xi

Part 1: Build

Chapter 1. Building With Structure 3

Chapter 2. Building the Formal Learning Experience 21

Chapter 3. Building the Informal Learning Experience 51

Chapter 4. Building the Learning Ecosystem 69

Part 2: Borrow

Chapter 5. Borrowing the Time and Talent of Others 87

Chapter 6. Borrowing Inspiration From Everywhere 99

Part 3: Buy

Chapter 7. Paying for Convenience 113

Chapter 8. Paying for an Extra Set of Hands 121

Chapter 9. Paying for Off-the-Shelf Instructional Design Solutions 129

Bringing It All Together 137

Appendix A. Tools and Templates 143

Appendix B. Worked Examples 161

References and Resources 171

Index 175

About the Author 185

About ATD 187

ABOUT THE
ON A
SHOESTRING
SERIES

ATD's On a Shoestring series helps professionals successfully execute core topics in training and talent development when facing limitations of time, money, staff, and other resources. This series was designed for practitioners who work as a department of one, for new or "accidental" trainers, instructional designers, and learning managers who need fast, inexpensive access to practical strategies that work, and for those who work for small organizations or in industries that have limited training and development resources. This book will help you whether you're new to instructional design or have a lot of experience but now must develop effective training programs with less time, support, and budget.

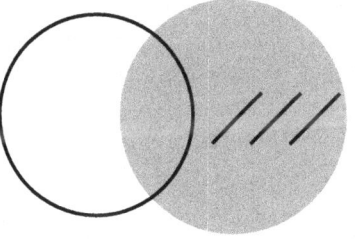

Introduction

"Do you believe in miracles?!"

In the 1980 Winter Olympics, a group of amateur college hockey players from the United States shocked the world by upsetting the Soviet Union's much more experienced, much more professional, and seemingly invincible hockey team. Some say it was the greatest upset in the history of sports. And as the clock wound down, Al Michaels's spontaneous and rhetorical question—"Do you believe in miracles?!"—captured the moment perfectly.

Whether you like sports or not, there are so many pieces of this story to learn from and admire. However, considering this is a book about instructional design, I'll go straight to the piece that is applicable for our purposes.

In 1980, the US men's Olympic hockey team fielded a group of amateur players from various colleges. They were given 11 months to come together and compete against teams that had been playing together for years. With comparatively little money, time, and experience, the team was operating on a shoestring, and it would truly require a miracle for them to make their mark on the world stage.

Do you ever feel like you're in a metaphorically similar situation? A situation in which you have few resources and yet are asked to develop some sort of training program or other learning initiative to help turn things around for your organization?

Do you need to design training programs on a shoestring?

I'm not sure this book will yield a 1980 Winter Olympic-sized miracle—on the scale of inspiring an entire generation of youth hockey players—but my hope is it can help you deliver smaller yet meaningful results for your organization. Every chapter, piece of content, and reproducible job aid has been designed to help you immediately apply basic (and sometimes advanced) concepts of instructional design when you're working with limited resources.

Introduction

Take great caution, however, when you begin to apply some of the principles in this book to your real-life situation. When you show that you can effectively design a learning program with few or no resources, people may begin to see you as something of a miracle worker, especially if your programs consistently demonstrate strategic thinking and high-quality design that aligns with proven principles of adult learning and offers results to key stakeholders. When you become known as a "learning-focused miracle worker," more people may come to you for help with their business or performance issues. And if you're already stretched thin with your existing work, this can be a daunting proposition, but it will help elevate you and the L&D function to higher levels, and perhaps present a business case for expanding beyond a department of one or a few.

So, keep reading only if you want to be perceived as the "miracle worker" for learning-focused design.

What This Book Isn't, and What It Is

Before I go further in introducing the concepts of instructional design on a shoestring, I want to be sure you know what's out of scope and in scope for this book.

This is not a resource that goes deep into instructional design models or theory. While I'll cover the basics of instructional design, I'll principally focus on the widely used ADDIE model of instructional design. ADDIE stands for analyze, design, develop, implement, and evaluate. In both academia and social media, people get very heated over its origins (Who gets credit for the model? Was it the US military or Florida State University?) and theoretical applications. While there is a time and place to get to the bottom of these arguments and ensure proper credit is given where it's due, when you're operating on a shoestring, it's neither the time nor place for such academic arguments.

DEEPER DIVE
Instructional Design Theory and Models

This book will discuss how the ADDIE model can be applied to give your learning programs structure; however, if you'd like to read more deeply about a specific theory or model of instructional design, you may wish to pick up one or more of these books:

xii

- Chuck Hodell, *ISD from the Ground Up: A No-Nonsense Approach to Instructional Design*, 4th ed. (Alexandria, VA: ATD Press, 2015).
- Julie Dirksen, *Design for How People Learn*, 2nd ed. (San Francisco: New Riders, 2016).
- Guy W. Wallace, *Performance-Based Lesson Mapping and Instructional Development Using a Facilitated Group Process* (2021).
- Megan Torrance, *Agile for Instructional Designers: Iterative Project Management to Achieve Results* (Alexandria, VA: ATD Press, 2019).
- Michael Allen and Richard Sites, *Leaving ADDIE for SAM: An Agile Model for Developing the Best Learning Experiences* (Alexandria, VA: ATD Press, 2012).

This book is a crash course in how to immediately apply a widely used instructional design model with projects you're currently working on (or will be working on soon). In alignment with sound principles of adult learning, I don't want you to simply read through these pages and nod and think to yourself: "That makes sense! Maybe I'll even use it next time I'm working on a training project."

If you're currently working on a project (or will be soon), I hope that the information, resources, and job aids will be helpful to you immediately. I want you to highlight key points. I want you to put some of these ideas into your own words and use them with your teams or project sponsors. I want you to put aside any discomfort you may have with writing in a book, and I want you to spend time filling out some of the job aids you'll find throughout.

Don't worry about ruining the job aids in this book. At your convenience, you can always download more at endurancelearning.com/books/shoestring or by using this QR code!

This book isn't focused solely on instructor-led training or e-learning development. Throughout this book, you'll find comments and examples of instructional design on a shoestring for in-person training; virtual sessions; asynchronous, self-guided e-learning programs; and everything in between. Many of the examples, resources, and job aids that you'll find in this book can be applied to all sorts of learning projects.

Introduction

This book is about figuring out what the best learning solution might be and whether learning is even the solution. This is important—there may be times when someone asks you to help develop a training program, but, if you're doing your analysis correctly, the problem you're looking to solve may not even be related to learning or professional development. Perhaps the root cause of the issue is a policy that encourages (or discourages) a particular behavior. Perhaps there are some systemic issues that can't be trained away.

In the following pages, you'll be introduced to an instructional design model that will give you some structure to work with and a variety of questions you can ask at each stage. Based on the answers to these questions and through the processes in this book, you'll be able to determine if training can help move the needle on whatever issue you need to address. You'll also ask questions that can help you decide how the learning initiative should be delivered. Should it be in-person? Virtual? E-learning? Should it just be a job aid? Can people simply Google the answer or find a solution on YouTube or search for it in your company's shared drive? Should there be prelearning? How will the learning content live on beyond the learning event?

Being able to answer these questions is what instructional design is all about.

This book will not give you an instructional design easy button. It's about instructional design on a shoestring, but the concepts and strategies you'll find throughout these pages will require some work on your end and some buy-in on the part of anyone who has requested your help in creating training programs.

Maybe you have encountered a version of this situation: "Your proposal makes a lot of sense. Unfortunately, it's not in our budget to do something like that. Instead of you presenting to the group, can you just show me what to do and then help me create a few resources that I can offer as handouts?"

Or maybe this one: "Yeah, I understand that you come from the L&D world and want to apply adult learning principles. You're suggesting a longer learning experience, but we don't have time for that. Can you just turn these slides into an e-learning course so we can get our people what they need?"

Or maybe even this one: "We already have all the content. Can you help us make our slides look better? And maybe help us add an activity or two so that the content is more engaging?"

Introduction

Each of these scenarios (and their infinite variations) features a request by someone who may have a sincere need but doesn't understand how effective learning works.

Someone with visual design skills can make a slide deck look infinitely better and more professional, but it doesn't mean that the deck will be delivered any more effectively. It doesn't mean that people will actually learn anything new or be able to do anything differently or better.

The right content can always be delivered quickly and directly, but it doesn't mean people will remember it or know what to do with it if they are in a situation in which they should be using it someday.

Sometimes Google or YouTube provides the easy button people need. Usually, however, if someone is requesting a training program, there are limited shortcuts that you can take and still be effective.

This book is about being effective, even with limited resources. If we're not effective in helping people do things differently or better, then we haven't done our jobs very well. Having limited time, money, or expertise—basically designing learning programs on a shoestring—can certainly be a challenge, but it's never an excuse that can absolve us of our most fundamental responsibility: to create effective learning experiences.

Did you notice that I've been using the word "effective," not "engaging"? That's an intentional word choice. *Effective* learning design is generally engaging, but more importantly, effective learning design means designing to achieve a specific outcome. *Engaging* learning design might mean that you're holding learners' attention, and they may even enjoy your learning experience, but engaging learning doesn't necessarily mean results are being achieved.

What Is Instructional Design?

Most of this introduction has revolved around the concept of developing learning experiences "on a shoestring" and the mechanics of this book. Of course, we can't jump into a book about instructional design on a shoestring without defining *instructional design*.

If you've read any learning industry articles, books, or social media posts, you've likely seen a bevy of terms (such as *instructional design, learning design,* or *learning experience design*) being used interchangeably, which can make them

xv

Introduction

very confusing. Perhaps you have your own ideas about or definition of instructional design in mind.

I'm a firm believer that if you have a definition for a given term, you should embrace it fully. I also believe that when lots of people define a term in different ways, any conversations about that term can only be productive if everyone agrees—if only for a short period—on one common definition.

For the purposes of this book, I'm asking you to put your own definition of instructional design on hold so that we can all agree to use this definition:

instructional design [in-**struhk**-shuhn-ul dih-**zahyn**]

noun

A practice by which learner or organizational learning needs are identified leading to a learning solution being crafted, implemented, evaluated, and refined.

Build, Borrow, or Buy: How to Use This Book

This book is structured to help your instructional design be *effective* in three ways, broken into three parts:

1. **Build.** The first four chapters of this book are what I call the "Do-It-Yourself" portion. In these chapters, you'll find information and resources to help you build the structure of your instructional design process (chapter 1), build an effective formal learning program (chapter 2), identify and intentionally build informal learning opportunities (chapter 3), and build an ecosystem that can support any of your learning initiatives (chapter 4). As with any do-it-yourself effort, these strategies are often applied when you're looking to save some money or when you think you have (or would like to develop) a certain skill set and want to be proud of what you've created. While you'll have more ownership and endless possibilities for customization when building your own learning programs, it typically requires more time and your programs may look less refined than other options.

2. **Borrow.** The middle two chapters of this book align with the adage: There are no new ideas, just recycled ones. In this part, you'll think through how best to use the time and talents of other people

Introduction

(chapter 5) as well as examine ways that others' work might inspire your training design (chapter 6). When you're able to effectively borrow time and expertise from others, and when you're open to gaining inspiration from anywhere, you might be able to save on the development costs or time for your project.

3. **Buy.** The last three chapters of this book might be the closest thing to an "easy button" you'll find, but pressing that button will often come with a cost. If you're operating on a shoestring because of a time crunch, but you have some funding available, then this part of the book—which offers ways to pay for convenience (chapter 7), an extra set of hands (chapter 8), and off-the-shelf content (chapter 9)—might be exactly what you need.

Your circumstances and the resources you have at your disposal will most likely determine what combination of *build, borrow,* and *buy* will best apply to your instructional design initiatives.

Recurring Elements

Throughout this book, you'll see icons marking four recurring elements:

 Time Saver: This is a strategy for shaving time off a best practice.

 On the Cheap: These are free or low-cost ideas and tools or suggestions for how to get funding.

 Deeper Dive: These are callout boxes throughout the text saying something like "Did this whet your appetite? Here's a resource to deepen your knowledge."

 Tool: This is a job aid, tool, or checklist to help you put ideas into action. You'll find tool callouts throughout the text and complete versions in appendix A.

You Can Do It—Even on a Shoestring

Perhaps you work for a small, mission-focused nonprofit organization that aspires to bring peace and harmony to a specific corner of the world. When practiced

Introduction

effectively, instructional design can make the difference between an initiative that saves the world and an initiative that wastes valuable time and money.

Perhaps you work for a huge global corporation and have been asked to redesign an element of compliance training. When practiced effectively, instructional design can make the difference between an initiative that helps someone do their job better (or stay out of trouble) and an initiative that people just groan and complain about. While it may not seem like much, people can spend more waking hours at their jobs during the week than they do with their families, so being able to do their jobs better (or simply stay out of trouble) can have profound effects on their lives.

This book offers you a structure and some models, resources, and job aids to help ensure that every instructional design project on which you embark—even (and especially) when on a shoestring—has the best chance of success. When you use the information, models, resources, or suggestions in these pages, I hope that the fog around a new and potentially daunting learning project may be lifted, and you'll feel more confident in developing the right solution for the time you have to deliver results, without breaking the bank.

PART 1
BUILD

In the first part of this book, you'll be able to explore the different do-it-yourself options that are available to you as you design learning experiences on a shoestring. In chapter 1, you'll discover what "instructional design" is. (Hint: It's more than just designing a slide deck or a lesson plan or building an e-learning module.) You'll also take a closer look at a commonly used instructional design model, which will offer you structure and a process for identifying the learning needs of your project, designing and developing the solution, and then deploying your solution and determining how successful it was.

In chapter 2, you'll find tools, resources, and a process for developing effective, engaging formal training programs—whether they are live, instructor-led experiences (like classroom training or webinars) or self-guided, asynchronous e-learning modules.

Remember that not all learning solutions will involve formal training programs. In fact, when you're operating on a shoestring, the best and most cost-effective way to help people learn or get the information they need is through less structured, informal learning experiences. Chapter 3 will focus on several informal learning experiences that you may want to intentionally build into the learning solutions you develop.

Finally, chapter 4 delves into the ecosystem you'll want to build to secure buy-in, form relationships, get help from early testers, and overcome barriers to learners accessing your resources.

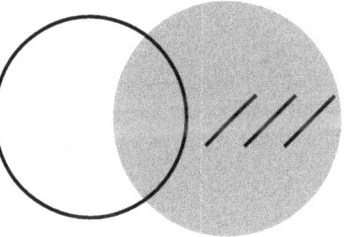

1
Building With Structure

My company's biggest client—a Fortune 500 manufacturing company—had just introduced us to a large, international wholesale club that needed to put together a training program. If we dazzled the training team at the wholesale club, we would have a major new client. If we fumbled the opportunity, we ran the risk of embarrassing our biggest client and damaging our most important relationship.

Because of the nature of our relationship with the manufacturing company, and the work we'd already done with them, we assumed that the project with this new potential client would be an instructor-led training program. During our initial call, we learned some things about the project, including the client's ultimate goals, the nature of the learners, and the limited opportunities to take employees off the floor for professional development purposes. That's when we realized our assumptions were wrong—in-person training wouldn't work in this environment and we'd need to create a hybrid learning experience. Frontline staff would only be able to access learning opportunities digitally; however, managers would have an opportunity to learn in-person, specifically how to support their frontline staff's professional development.

When someone reaches out to tell me that they think they need training, I get excited and want to jump right in to develop a creative, fun, and engaging learning program. Perhaps that feeling of excitement and an opportunity to show people how creative and engaging training can be resonates with you. But, in my example, if we hadn't first spent several hours with some of the key stakeholders to determine what was driving their desire for training and to learn more about the learners themselves, we would have proposed (and developed)

Chapter 1

an absolutely beautiful, engaging training program that nobody would have actually been able to use.

Having a structure for your instructional design efforts provides the best opportunity possible to ensure that learning is the answer to the challenge or opportunity in front of you and ensures the solution you propose is the most well-thought-out, best possible initiative to achieve the results you're looking for.

What Is "Instructional Design Structure"?

First, it's important to clarify the difference between *instructional design structure* and *strategies for designing instruction*.

An *instructional design structure* is a model that can help guide you through the entire process of identifying learning needs, crafting an appropriate solution, and then implementing, evaluating, and refining that solution. On the other hand, *strategies for designing instruction*—which can sometimes be referred to as "instructional design models" (because they're technically models for designing instruction)—are just one step in the middle of the bigger, classical instructional design process.

We'll go into some strategies for designing instruction that are rooted in adult learning theory in the next chapter, but keep in mind that just because you're adept at putting together an engaging slide deck, lesson plan, or e-learning module, it doesn't mean you're doing instructional design. Someone who is using instructional design structure consistently goes through an entire process, from needs analysis through the refinement of the learning solution.

DEEPER DIVE
Instructional Design Models

If you'd like a brief history of instructional design models, Angel Green offers an easily digestible chapter in *ATD's Handbook for Training and Talent Development* (2022) titled "ADDIE: The Origin of Modern-Day ISD." She points out that "Having a solid understanding of instructional theory will help in your design, but without a process to follow, you can't build an instructional product. On the other hand, simply using a model without an understanding of learning theory can push a product through to creation, but the product likely won't be appropriately designed (or instructionally sound)."

4

The most referenced instructional design model is the ADDIE model, which stands for analyze, design, develop, implement, and evaluate. If you do a Google search for the phrase "instructional design model," you'll find myriad models that are popular today, including SAM (successive approximation model) and LLAMA (lot like Agile management approach). Perhaps you've been exposed to or have used another model. I'd argue that all reputable instructional design models in use today are a variation of ADDIE, so that is the model we'll be referring to as we navigate the remainder of this chapter.

How Do You Build With Structure?

Using a structured model for instructional design is so important, especially for projects on a shoestring, because it offers a consistent, replicable way to organize a learning initiative. Structure helps ensure the purpose and audience are clear and the instructional approach will meet the needs of your client in a sound manner. Every time.

How can ADDIE help? I like to think of it as an organized way to ask questions and challenge assumptions about a potential learning initiative. Figure 1-1 offers some actions you can take in each step of this instructional design model. These ideas may help you begin working on your next learning initiative, as you navigate each step of the ADDIE model and apply it to your solution. However, while it may be helpful, this is not intended to be an exhaustive list. You may have your own questions that you use on a training intake form, or you may find other useful ideas by searching the internet. Of course, if time is one of your resource constraints while on a shoestring, these actions will help you get started.

TIME SAVER
Getting It Right From the Beginning

Going through the ADDIE process can save you both time and money by ensuring you settle on the best possible solution and preventing rework. Undoubtedly, there will be projects that you'll be asked to turn around quickly, but if you don't invest time in getting it right from the beginning, you may find that your learning solution isn't as effective as it could have been (which is a waste of money) or you may need to redo some or all of your learning solution down the road (which is a waste of time and money).

Chapter 1

Figure 1-1. Actions to Take When Using ADDIE

A Analyze	• Ask questions and challenge assumptions. • Determine the best design path forward.
D Design	• Apply a design model (such as anchor, content, application, and future use) that fits the delivery medium, audience needs, and other elements uncovered during analysis. • Create lesson plans or storyboards. • Revise as needed.
D Develop	• Review and evaluate the design to make this a real learning experience. • Bring the design to life with actual materials, guides, or e-learning assets. • Perform Q&A. • Revise as needed.
I Implement	• Ideally, run a pilot phase first. • Deliver instruction or load materials into an LMS. • Gather feedback. • Review (initial) results. • Revise as needed.
E Evaluate	• Collect data on delivery and performance. • Revise as needed.

Analyze

In the first step of the ADDIE process, you're on a fact-finding mission, asking questions and challenging assumptions to determine as much as you can about the root cause of the learning need, which can help you identify whether learning is a solution for the issue. In this step, you'll also want to learn as much as you can about your target audience to determine how they'll be able to consume any solution you propose.

> **Question:** What problem do we want to solve, or what opportunity can we build upon?

> **Questions behind the question:** What's driving the request for training? Individual performance? Group, team, or organizational performance? Is the requested training program less about performance or skill building and more about team building?

Building With Structure

Answers to these questions may help reveal if training is really the answer. It's not uncommon for a request for training to be solved with a job aid, meeting, or change to the organizational structure or process. In addition, if you learn that a training program is being requested for team building purposes, your success metric may be less about measurable outcomes and more about team dynamics, which you'll want to keep in mind as you design the experience.

Question: How do we know it's a problem (or opportunity)?

Questions behind the question: Do we have any data that can help us determine if it's a real or perceived problem? Do we have any baseline data that we could compare with post-training results to determine if the initiative moved the needle? Are we even sure that training or some sort of learning initiative will help solve the problem?

Don't be surprised (and don't panic) if you can't find hard and fast data showing the need. Most organizations know there is a problem or need before they can prove it. Ask these questions to begin collecting data that can, if only anecdotally, offer the hypothesis of a challenge and a hint at what stakeholders would like to see change.

Question: What would happen if we did nothing?

Questions behind the question: Is it worth our time to put together a learning initiative? How urgent is this request?

Question: What do we know about the target audience?

Questions behind the question: Is everyone all in one place (which is more conducive to in-person training)? Are people dispersed across offices, regions, or continents (which makes an in-person solution less feasible)? Is everyone of the same literacy level (which will affect the design of visual aids, learning materials, and learning activities)? If we're considering a digital solution, will people be going through the learning experience on computers, tablets, or smartphones?

You see where this is going. The more you know about the audience, the better customized the learning solution will be for them. You may think you know

Chapter 1

the answers to many of these questions, but an elite instructional designer does not assume they know everything about their audience. Simply discussing the audience will ultimately help everyone align and may help you challenge your own or your team's assumptions. Even when facing the pressures of operating on a shoestring, making assumptions can lead to unnecessary rework, poor results, or both.

Question: If training is part of the proposed solution, what barriers or resistance could we encounter?

Questions behind the question: If we redesign or replace an existing training program, will the original designers be upset? Will some learners think that they already know the information and are being forced to take the training course because some people on the team aren't performing? What challenges could occur when taking people offline (away from their jobs) to complete the training program? Do learners think that they've been trained and know what to do, but aren't being supported in other ways?

Question: At the end of the day, what will have changed based on this learning initiative, and how will we know? How will success be defined and measured for this initiative?

Question behind the question: A year from now, if someone walked up to you and said, "Wow, that training initiative was so successful!" what evidence could they give you to indicate it was indeed successful?

Question: What is the timeline for this project?

Questions behind the question: What is driving the timeline? Do we have time to create lots of visually attractive materials, or are we just hoping to get the information into the hands of the people? Do we have time to bring in creative case studies or branching scenarios, or will we need to find less technical but no less engaging ways to present the material?

Question: Who and where will the content come from?

Questions behind the question: Will there be one subject matter expert (SME) or multiple? Is source material available or does it need to be created? Who will need to approve the content? Will there be differing or competing perspectives on the content that will be difficult to resolve?

The analyze component of ADDIE is where most of the questions need to be asked so that whatever learning initiative you design (assuming that you've confirmed a learning initiative will help with the problem) will be focused, on target, and delivered in the most appropriate way. However, there are still a handful of questions you'll want to keep in mind at other points in the instructional design process.

One shortcoming of ADDIE (and any other model) is that it needs to be represented in a 2D fashion on paper, and when people look at any ADDIE diagram, they may mistakenly think there's a linear nature to it. While I'm placing additional questions under the "DDIE" portions of ADDIE, you may find it useful to ask them during your analysis (or during other stages of your project where they'd be more helpful). You may also want to ask them more than once as your instructional design project unfolds and evolves.

DEEPER DIVE
Needs Assessments

For more on the analyze component of ADDIE, and uncovering the need behind a training request, check out another book in this series: *Needs Assessment on a Shoestring* by Kelly Jones and Jody Lumsden.

Design

In the design step, you begin to sketch what the learning solution will be, based on what you uncovered during the analysis. For example, this step may include a lesson plan for an instructor-led training course or a storyboard for an e-learning solution. The questions you ask in the design step will help refine your learning

Chapter 1

objectives (or create subobjectives) and clarify the degree of mastery that learners will be expected to achieve.

Question: How will stakeholders (SMEs, project sponsors, and so on) be engaged?

Questions behind the question: Should there be regularly scheduled meetings? Who needs to provide feedback or sign off on the solution?

As you begin to draft what the learning solution will look like, get feedback from all key players before you take your design too far. There are few things worse in the instructional design process than getting far along on a project only to hear, "Oh wait, our team lead wasn't included in the initial reviews, but they have strong opinions and would like to make a dozen changes!"

Question: What should people be able to do differently or better as a result of this project?

Questions behind the question: What behaviors will people need to begin, improve, or change, and how can they be written as learning objectives or outcomes? Are there specific activities, exercises, assessments, or simulations we should be thinking of that will be directly tied to these behaviors and skills?

Question: Is awareness or skill development the ultimate outcome, or is it not learning related (such as team building)?

Questions behind the question: Will a simple job aid suffice? Can the goals be accomplished in a single event (a training session or an e-learning module)? Should the initiative include a mix of formal elements (training sessions and e-learning modules) and informal elements (resources, job aids, post-training mentoring, or a drip campaign with regular reminders and content)?

Question: What success metrics will be evaluated, and how will that information be collected?

Building With Structure

Question behind the question: How do we bake the (various levels of) evaluation into the project's design from the start and not leave it until the end?

Getting good answers to these questions will help ensure your learning solution is spot on, and you'll spend less time staring blankly at your screen, wondering exactly what kind of activity you should include in a certain section. With these questions, you may need to help your client improve upon and refine their answers. "They need to understand X" or "They need to know all this information" are common thoughts that clients express, and it'll be your responsibility to help them be more specific. Asking for clarity can help you and your client stay on the same page. I've found this comment helps clients elaborate: "OK, let's finish that sentence. They really need to understand X so that they can do what?"

Question: Is the design inclusive of all learners?

Questions behind the question: What accessibility considerations and measures will be integrated into the design? Will all learners be able to connect with the imagery, details of examples and case studies, or other content?

Question: What is the best way to get the learners what they need?

Questions behind the question: If the learners are dispersed, should we design e-learning content or live, virtual programs? Will a simple job aid solve the problem? Will any materials need to be translated or localized? How are adult learning principles being integrated into the design?

Thinking about how learners will access your solution should be integrated into your design process at the earliest stages. Whether you're talking about accessibility for learners to ensure your solution is compliant with Web Content Accessibility Guidelines (WCAG), or you're talking about learners who will be accessing your solution in a low-bandwidth region or on their phones, these are all factors that will influence your design.

Chapter 1

Question: Who will deliver the session (if we design an instructor-led training program)?

Questions behind the question: How many different facilitators will there be? Will the program be delivered by the same person who designed it? How experienced and dynamic are the facilitators? Will it be delivered in-person or virtually?

Question: Where will this program live (if we design an e-learning solution)?

Questions behind the question: What will we need to keep in mind when loading the program onto a learning management system (LMS)? Will high-bandwidth assets (like videos) cause issues?

Develop

Everything comes to life in the develop phase. This is when you'll have a better understanding of whether the activities, instructions, interactions, and talking points in your lesson plan or storyboard will actually work. You'll also begin to determine if the amount of time you allocated for an activity or the interaction you sketched in a storyboard is realistic. It's also the stage at which you can begin to show real pieces of your learning solution to whomever requested it to get their feedback on the look and feel of it, as well as their thoughts on what the activities will look like in real life.

Question: Who will be involved in the development?

Questions behind the question: Will there be a team (instructional designer, graphic designer, and developer), or will one person be putting everything together? If more than one person, how will deadlines be communicated, and what version control measures need to be put in place?

Question: What quality assurance (QA) measures or processes need to be put in place?

Building With Structure

Questions behind the question: How do we make sure we don't deliver final materials that have typos, grammatical errors, or incorrect information? How will we make sure navigation or links in an e-learning module are not broken?

From grammar and spelling checks or inaccurate page references in a participant guide to broken "next" buttons in an e-learning module, it's easy to miss simple mistakes. Having a clearly defined QA process (or a checklist) can help ensure your final product looks and feels professional.

Question: When will the development of the project be deemed complete?

Question behind the question: Will there be an initial pilot program to collect data or make observations that lead to adjustments to the materials?

This is an extremely important question to ensure expectations are aligned. If you're prepared to make one set of edits but your client expects unlimited revisions, then you may experience frustration checking this project off your to-do list so that you can move on to the next one.

Implement

You debut your learning solution for the world to see in the implement phase. Depending on the size and complexity of the solution, you may wish to implement it in stages, through an initial pilot or alpha test with a small group of learners to work out the kinks and to refine your product.

Question: How will the final files be turned over to key stakeholders?

Questions behind the question: Does everyone have access to and knowledge of how to use the technologies involved in creating the materials? If we design an e-learning program, how will SCORM files be shared and uploaded to the LMS?

13

Chapter 1

Whether you're turning over PowerPoint decks or SCORM packages, your files may be too big to email. Having a plan for how to deliver the files to your client so they can easily access them will make everyone's life a little easier.

Question: How will facilitators be prepared to deliver the program (if we design an instructor-led training program)?

Questions behind the question: Will there be a train-the-trainer session? What will facilitators need to demonstrate to show they can proficiently deliver the program with fidelity?

If you are not delivering the training program that you've developed, you'll want to be sure other trainers understand the rhyme and reason behind the sequence and flow of your program.

Evaluate

While you should be testing your solution throughout this process, the evaluate phase is your opportunity to determine whether your learning solution is meeting the business's or learners' needs. This phase often takes place over time—from post-training feedback through follow-up to know what behaviors are changing on the job and how performance challenges are being addressed. The data collected here can help you further refine your learning solution as well as allow you to demonstrate the value of your program to key stakeholders.

Question: Did the program do what we intended? How do we know?

Questions behind the question: Beyond any evaluation and assessment strategies integrated into the program's design, what other data or information needs to be collected? What story is the data from this program telling us?

What Does Build With Structure Look Like in Practice?

Now that we've gotten some foundational concepts out of the way, let's explore what using the ADDIE model looks like in real life. The following case studies are based on actual instructional design projects that my company has worked on. They illustrate the importance of using a model to gather information so that the final product has the highest possible chance of doing what we set out to accomplish.

Example 1. "We Need Training"

Let's return to the initial example from earlier in this chapter. A client introduced us to a large wholesale club that was interested in having a training program built to help their retail sales staff. This was all that we knew heading into our first meeting with the potential client. Because we had primarily created instructor-led, in-person training solutions for the client that had introduced us, we assumed that we would be creating another instructor-led, in-person training project.

Analysis

When we began to ask the wholesale club's training director some questions, we learned several things that quickly had us discarding our initial assumptions. First, we learned that there was a clear business case for this training program (a small increase in sales for a specific department would lead to an enormous difference in the company's bottom line). Second, we learned that the primary audience for the training program would be thousands of retail staff working in locations across North America. They would not be able to come together in-person, nor would they be able to take much time away from their workstations, as they had a constant flow of customers. Department managers, however, sometimes came together in-person at a central training location for professional development.

Design

Based upon our initial analysis, we proposed a two-pronged approach to this training challenge:

- Create a series of short e-learning modules that revolved around a standard sales process and provided product information for frontline retail staff.
- Create a multiday, in-person supervisor training program for department managers. It would offer some general leadership development strategies (because many of these department managers

were first-time managers) as well as some specific strategies for how these managers could reinforce what the frontline retail staff would learn during the e-learning modules.

While we had a solid framework for the design of this program that was approved by the project sponsor, we also realized we needed to revisit the analysis step in our process to do more fact-finding. This is such an important point to anyone using the ADDIE model that I will repeat it here: **Even though on paper ADDIE appears to be a linear model, it is OK (and often necessary) to return to a previous step based upon the project's needs.**

For further fact-finding, one of our team members visited several high-performing wholesale clubs to observe and learn more about what they were doing well and the kind of sales process they were using. This in-person study of authentic behaviors and on-the-job performance was more valuable than any information we may have been able to glean from a SME or existing materials about sales processes. Of course, we were fortunate that a handful of clubs were all located within several hours driving distance of one of our team members. When you're working on a shoestring, you may not have the resources to fly or travel to observe what's happening on-site, but finding ways to access and learn from people—through a phone or video call—who are in the roles your training solution is focused on (from a variety of locations that may be high performing or otherwise) is truly invaluable.

Development

Once we completed the storyboards (for the e-learning modules) and lesson plans (for the in-person components), we developed the e-learning modules and instructor-led materials. In addition, we created a train-the-trainer program to help all facilitators understand the breadth of the e-learning modules and ensure they would be comfortable delivering the in-person manager training with fidelity to the curriculum.

Implementation

We conducted the train-the-trainer program, trained an initial cohort of managers, and uploaded the e-learning modules to the organization's LMS. Based on lessons learned in both the train-the-trainer program and the initial manager training cohort, we made several changes and updates to the materials.

Evaluation

Data we collected about the number of frontline retail staff completing the e-learning modules and anecdotal feedback about the manager training cohort indicated that the program was achieving what it set out to achieve: more knowledgeable sales associates with improved capacity to educate their members and more engaged supervisors with higher awareness of the need to support their frontline salesforce.

Example 2. "We Need Training"

No, that's not a typo. I didn't just copy and paste a case study template and then forget to change the title. This project began with the exact same three-word request that you read about in the previous example. The result, however, was very different.

The CEO of a small but rapidly growing construction company shared with me that her company's staff had more than doubled over the past year. While the organization originally consisted of only a handful of extremely experienced professionals, who knew the niche nature of the business very well, the expansion meant there were many more junior staffers who lacked experience and knowledge about some of the core tasks that clients hired the company to perform. The CEO thought she needed help with the design of some short training modules that could be delivered virtually, and she was particularly interested in getting help with some strategies to engage people through virtual training.

Analysis

To learn more about the business and individual needs for a professional development initiative, I set up a series of one-on-one interviews with a handful of junior and senior employees. I quickly learned that the professional development needs for just about every individual were very different. While training and professional development in some way, shape, or form might eventually be helpful, it didn't appear to me that training would solve the most immediate problem that I found during the analysis step.

Design

During the analysis, we learned that people across the organization didn't have a common understanding of what they should be really good at, so developing

Chapter 1

training at this point might lead us to miss the mark on what individuals or the organization as a whole would need.

I talked with the CEO and her executive team about first developing a common set of competencies that people across the organization should have proficiency in, and outlining to what degree, based upon their role and level in the organization. The CEO and the executive team agreed, so I returned to the analysis phase to conduct interviews with staff across the organization and learn more about what collections of knowledge, skills, and abilities led to success in the organization.

If this process was linear, I would have already completed the interviews. So, I'll say it again: **ADDIE is not a linear process.** Before I could design an effective competency model, I needed to talk with the staff again. This time I asked different questions because the learning solution's objective had changed from "We need training" to "We need to know what we should train people on."

Development

Following the interviews, I designed and developed a competency framework. The framework isolated a set of competencies that everyone across the organization needed to demonstrate proficiency in, as well as several additional competencies related to people management that were specific to senior-level staff.

The people management competencies were important because, prior to this project, everyone in the organization reported directly to the CEO. As the company grew, this was no longer sustainable. In addition, employee development needs were diverse, so general training sessions wouldn't work. We explored connecting several junior-level staff members with a senior-level staff member in a mentoring relationship. However, we realized we would now need to design and develop a mentor training program for senior-level staff as well as a general training session for all staff on participating in a mentoring program.

With this in mind, we again broke the linear nature of ADDIE and returned to the design phase to put this part of the learning initiative together.

Implementation

Once the materials were prepared, the organization held a virtual session with all staff to help increase their awareness of the overall structure of their future professional development (from the rollout of the competency model to the

Building With Structure

introduction of the mentor-mentee pairings). The organization also conducted a session for senior staff to help them better understand the mentor role and grow familiar with how to use the competency model.

Evaluation

While this project began with the phrase "We need training," it didn't directly result in training, at least not in the traditional sense. The initial request was more about virtual presentation delivery training and how to put together brown-bag lunch sessions. The result was less about training sessions and more about how to help individuals across the organization get the specific assistance and development coaching they needed.

Just over a year after the program's launch, a survey of employees revealed that 100 percent of mentees agreed or strongly agreed with the statement: "I find the conversations with my mentor to be a good use of my time." However, some mentors expressed discomfort with their mentor role. Based on this data, we provided mentors with additional support measures, including training and job aids, to continue increasing their effectiveness. In addition, the CEO and executive team began using the competency model to better pinpoint individual learning needs (which can be addressed by mentors) as well as trends in learning needs across the organization, which will eventually result in more formal training opportunities.

TOOL
Putting ADDIE to Work

This chapter is intended to provide you with an opportunity to put these concepts to use in real time. Perhaps you have a project that you've been working on. (Maybe that's even why you decided to buy this book!) Perhaps there's a past project that still stands out in your mind that you think might have gone better if you had given it some structure.

Either way, if you truly want to test how using a structure like the ADDIE model can help you with your programs, take a few minutes before you go on to the next chapter and try answering the questions in appendix A.

I'm serious; take out a pen (or pencil or marker) and physically write out your answers to the questions.

19

Chapter 1

A Shoestring Summary

While you can find several different structures for building your instructional design, every reputable instructional design model revolves around ADDIE. Using a structure like ADDIE can offer a big-picture view of your project and provide an organized and methodical way to ask questions and build your learning program. When you're operating on a shoestring, having a method you can apply repeatedly takes the guess work out of how to proceed after each step.

ADDIE may appear linear and 2D on paper, but the instructional design process should be dynamic, and a good instructional designer should not be afraid to revisit previous steps in the process as needed. This iterative component is important when you need to move fast because you don't have a lot of time or when you're juggling multiple projects and requests at once.

Spending time on each step and asking the right questions can help your project move forward smoothly, saving you time and money in the long run. If you're not asking the right questions, you might risk building the wrong solution, and that's not a mistake you can afford when you're working on a shoestring.

2
Building the Formal Learning Experience

When it's time to build a learning experience on a shoestring, the absolute worst thing you can do is open PowerPoint or another presentation software and start creating slides. Being short on money, time, or both doesn't mean that your instructional design needs to suffer.

I've heard some people say, "Well, a bad training course is better than no training," but this isn't true. Poor training can waste people's time (and in business, time generally translates into money). Poor training can also taint the reputation of future training initiatives by breaking your learners' trust, ensuring that anything you generate in the future will be of limited value.

In fact, here are 10 reasons not to make "opening PowerPoint" the first step in building your learning experience:

- If you haven't mapped out your learning experience first, how do you know you're putting the right content on each slide?
- PowerPoint is a linear visual tool operating in a world that insists on dynamic presentations.
- You'll likely just put a lot of words on each slide.
- You might tell yourself that you'll come back and make your slides better later, but as soon as you finish your slide deck, you'll probably move on to the next demand for your time.
- Everyone who hasn't yet read this book is opening PowerPoint first to create their presentation. Don't you want to be different than them?
- You can still put together slides later. First, decide on your sequence and flow, and then figure out if and where slides can help make your learning experience more powerful.

21

Chapter 2

- You'll spend too much time tinkering with fonts and designing your slides and not enough time thinking about how to connect your activities to your learning objectives.
- You may miss out on multiple methods for presenting information in an engaging way that doesn't include using slides.
- What will you do if your PowerPoint file is corrupted and won't open on the day of your presentation?
- Depending on what you're presenting and how you'd like to present it, you may discover that you don't even need slides!

Close PowerPoint for now. It can be a very important and powerful tool, but when you're designing on a shoestring, you don't have much margin for error. And the bottom line is that opening PowerPoint as your default first step is a big error.

The next question is, "Can you be ruthless?"

Can You Be Ruthless?

When you're short on money or time, you can't be a softy, and when it's time to build a learning experience on a shoestring, you will need to be absolutely ruthless. For example, you might have to decide whether to cut content from the learning program that you or the SME are emotionally attached to.

TOOL

How Ruthless Are You?

Think you have what it takes? Try the "How Ruthless Are You?" quiz in appendix A to learn where you fall on the "ruthless spectrum."

Some of you may be thinking: "This idea of being 'ruthless' makes me uncomfortable." Perhaps you equate being ruthless with being a jerk. That's fair. But I'm using ruthless to describe someone who is comfortable setting boundaries and saying no when there is a suggestion or an idea that doesn't align with the agreed-upon priorities, objectives, and outcomes. This doesn't make you a jerk.

I know some people who know how to say no very politely (yet firmly). They are ruthless. I know other people who are afraid to say no, so they agree to things that will bloat a training program. While their intentions may be good, their inability to say no can sink the effectiveness of the training program whether they're on a shoestring or not.

Keep in mind that when being ruthless, you're not always saying no to other people. Often, you'll have to say no to yourself, too. You'll have to get comfortable saying no to yourself even when you think you have a clever activity that might be fun. You'll have to say no to yourself even if you think the learners might appreciate some additional history or theory behind something.

What Happens If You Can't Be Ruthless?

The short answer: It's not good.

Here's some feedback I received when I latched onto an idea and turned into a big softy toward myself and my idea: "While I think everyone in this session appreciated the idea of the game you built for us, we just needed some information. We just needed a nice, reliable Ford Focus to get us where we needed to be, and you tried giving us a self-driving Tesla that sang Christmas songs every time we used the turn signal."

When you're building a learning experience on a shoestring, this is not the feedback you want to hear. In this example, rebuilding this training session would have put us on a second or third shoestring when we barely had the resources to build it on a single one.

But rebuild we did. My colleague and I had been pushing hard to develop a training session that revolved around a board game. We thought it would be fun because the focus of the session was on nonprofit board development. We made a training session that revolved around a "board" board game!

A fun idea indeed, but we should have been more ruthless. Instead, we misjudged the audience and what they needed from the training. We learned the hard way that when you're designing training solutions on a shoestring, every idea needs to be challenged.

TIME SAVER
Shortcut to Being Ruthless

When setting out to build any type of learning experience, you should constantly ask these questions: Is this necessary? Will this get us where we want to go in the most efficient and effective way possible?

Chapter 2

How Can You Ruthlessly Build Your Learning Experience?

A well-built, effective learning experience—regardless of your funding or the amount of time you have to create it—always comes down to your purpose or intent. Why do people need to learn something? To have greater awareness? To master a new skill? Do they need to learn it right now, or will people need to learn on demand at different times?

Aligning your learning solution's intent with the kind of learning experience you design (such as a training course, job aid, or stretch assignment with coaching) can help you save time, money, and effort. When you're building on a shoestring, you don't want to spend time designing a formal course if the appropriate learning experience may be a simple job aid or coaching.

What Is Your Intent?

When building a learning experience, you can't simply say, "As you wish!" when someone says, "We need training." As you learned from the examples in chapter 1, it's our responsibility as instructional designers to dig deeper and figure out why someone believes they need training.

Sometimes people have a very specific reason in mind when they request training. Sometimes they don't. You'll need to determine the goals, outcomes, and objectives, but you shouldn't use "trainer speak" to get there. No one outside an ATD meeting will give you a sound answer rooted in instructional design practices if you ask the question: "What are your learning objectives?"

So, it'll be important to learn more about the issue, challenge, or what people should be able to do. Let's dive deeper into some common reasons people say, "We need training."

Table 2-1 may help you quickly determine what kind of learning experience you should build based on someone's intent. Keep in mind that while this table may serve as a reference guide, it is not intended to be a complete list of the intent behind every learning need, nor is it an exhaustive list of every type of learning delivery method.

Building the Formal Learning Experience

Table 2-1. Matching Intent and Delivery Options

Request Intent	Suggested Delivery Options
Initial awareness or information sharing: • Providing new employee orientation • Introducing a new policy or procedure	• Job aid • Microlearning • Introduction or explainer video
New skill building: • Training first-time managers • Conducting computer system training • Training staff on a sales model • Providing coaching or mentoring training	• Job aid • Microlearning • Course (e-learning or instructor-led) • Tutorial
Advanced skill building: • Training a general surgeon on a new or advanced technique • Using code or advanced features to build custom interactions in an off-the-shelf software package	• Course (e-learning or instructor-led) • Hands-on work or stretch assignment with feedback or coaching
Remind and refresh: • Revisiting a policy or procedure to address the error rate • Meeting annual compliance requirements	• Job aid • Follow-up or drip campaign • Video • Article or document • Game
Change management: • Adopting a new IT system • Restructuring the organization • Rolling out new quality standards or standard operating procedures (SOPs)	• Communication campaign • Microlearning • Course (e-learning or instructor-led)
Just-in-time or on-demand: • Rolling out a new employee orientation • Supporting occasionally used processes or technical procedures • Completing forms or templates	• Job aid • Video • Article • E-learning course • Tutorial

Chapter 2

Table 2-1. Matching Intent and Delivery Options (Cont.)

Request Intent	Suggested Delivery Options
Prework: • Delivering content that is essential for learner knowledge alignment or for learners to be ready to engage in activities in advance of an instructor-led training course • Generating curiosity or enthusiasm for a larger learning initiative	• Video • E-learning course • Virtual, instructor-led training • Microlearning • Article with focused reflection questions
Post-training follow-up: • Providing resources and reminders to increase the likelihood learners will apply what they've learned • Completing certification	• Job aid • Follow-up or drip campaign • Video • Virtual, instructor-led training • Microlearning • Application assignments and reports

What Are Your Options?

Once you've determined the intent behind the learning need, it's time to build the learning experience itself. The following section will serve as a guide with helpful hints, templates, and reproducible materials to help you build your own formal learning program on a shoestring.

The next few pages will focus specifically on instructor-led training programs. If you're looking specifically for help with designing e-learning programs on a shoestring, you may want to skip ahead to the "Building a Learning Experience That Includes E-Learning" section.

Then, in chapter 3, we'll discuss specific ideas for building informal learning experiences.

Building a Learning Experience That Includes Instructor-Led Training

Instructor-led training (ILT) may be perhaps the most common type of formal learning experience in the workplace—people are learning informally all the

26

time by doing things like using Google or YouTube and asking more experienced co-workers for help.

Live (synchronous) ILT is usually delivered through two formats:

- In an in-person classroom
- Virtually via a web conferencing platform

I began this chapter by imploring you not to simply open PowerPoint when you've determined that ILT is an appropriate solution. I gave you 10 reasons not to open PowerPoint. You've now reached the point in the chapter where I share the first step you *should take*.

When building ILT programs, I recommend starting with a lesson plan that captures basic details as well as learning objectives, materials, estimated time, content, and instructional technique.

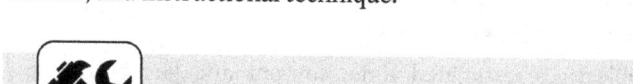

TOOL

Lesson Plan for Instructor-Led Training

In appendix A, you'll find a lesson plan template that I've shared with thousands of people to help them better organize their learning experiences in alignment with sound instructional design practices.

Let's explore how a lesson plan can best be used, component by component. The title, goal, date and time, and materials portions of the lesson plan are self-explanatory, but they shouldn't be overlooked:

- **Title.** Do you want your title to be straightforward, such as "Introduction to Using Salesforce"? Do you want it to reflect the value and importance of your course, such as "An Introduction to How We Boost Sales Through Salesforce"? Or do you want to set a lighter, approachable, even cheeky tone by calling it something like "Six Salesforce Selling Strategies Securing Stupendous Success"? The title of your ILT experience may be the first thing many learners see, and as the saying goes, you never get a second chance to make a first impression.
- **Goal.** This can be related to your intent. Your goal should summarize the big picture of what your ILT experience is supposed to do, help with, or address.

Chapter 2

- **Date and time.** Perhaps your ILT program will take place on a certain day at a certain time. Including the date and time can serve as a good reminder for anyone using the lesson plan. Perhaps this will be a recurring ILT experience that is two hours long and will take place every other month. In that case, you can use this part of the lesson plan to simply remind yourself how much time you have when designing your experience and to remind anyone else using it how much time they will have to deliver the experience.
- **Materials.** This section can be filled in as you design the lesson plan. When you insert an activity that requires sticky notes, markers, or handouts, add those items under the "Materials" section. Having all your materials listed in one spot will help ensure you don't forget anything heading into the training session.

The learning objectives, estimated time, content and key points, and instructional technique are all parts of your ILT experience that can be trickier to get right. Let's look at each of these sections in more depth.

Learning Objectives

Different from your overall goal and intent, the *learning objectives* of any learning experience should be framed in terms of what your learners should be able to do differently or better as a result of the experience. When creating learning objectives, think of finishing this sentence: "By the end of this training session, my learners will be able to . . ."

A well-crafted learning objective will relate to your intent, and if you spend a few minutes getting your learning objectives right, then your lesson plan should be much easier to write.

If your intent is for your staff to be aware of a new expense reimbursement policy, then perhaps your learning objective would be, "By the end of this training session, my learners will be able to locate the new reimbursement policy and requirements in the employee handbook." Because you've framed this objective in a way that describes your ideal learner behavior, you should have an easy path to creating this learning experience. Maybe you will say a few words about the new policy, but that's not enough information to meet your learning objective. You've said that the learners should be able to locate the policy in their

28

Building the Formal Learning Experience

employee handbook. If that's the actual objective, then you should also leave some time in the session to determine if your learners can indeed find the new policy in their handbooks.

However, if your intent is for your staff to gain more than just a general awareness and learn an actual skill, then you'll need a different learning objective. Perhaps you want to make sure people on your team are correctly filling out the reimbursement forms according to the new policy. This is different from simply knowing about the policy. In this case, your learning objective would be for your learners to be able to fill out the new reimbursement form with zero errors. There's a major difference between these learning objectives, and it relates to your intent. Once you have your learning objective, then the actual training experience is mostly mapped out. In this instance, perhaps you'd talk about the new policy and make sure people know where to find more information as well as where to locate the appropriate forms. But that's not all. You said you wanted people to accurately fill out the forms, so you need to leave some time in the session for people to practice filling out the form and for you to check their work and offer feedback.

DEEPER DIVE
Effective Learning Objectives

Learning objectives are the heart of any learning program and provide direction and guidance to keep it tight and focused. Any time one of my team members is stuck and not sure how to proceed with the development of a training course, my first question is usually, "What are the learning objectives?" This simple question helps, more times than not, get my colleagues unstuck.

If you'd like to learn more about crafting effective learning objectives, you should spend a little time with these resources:
- Will Thalheimer, "Learning Objectives—A Research-Inspired Odyssey," Work-Learning Research, video, January 29, 2015, youtu.be/PRX1RwxybCs.
- Brian Washburn, "Writing Effective Learning Objectives," *Train Like You Listen*, podcast, January 26, 2022, endurancelearning.com/blog/writing-effective-learning-objectives.

Chapter 2

Estimated Time

This column in the lesson plan is deceptively tricky. While you need not map out every minute of your presentation, you should intentionally break it up into chunks. Take a look at the lesson plan segment in Table 2-2.

Table 2-2. Estimating Time

Estimated Time	Content and Key Points	Instructional Technique
30 minutes	Introduce new policy: • Walk through new reimbursement policy • Form activity • Debrief	• Lecture • Individual activity • Discussion

Even if you were familiar with the new policy, do you think you'd be able to pick up this lesson plan and budget your time well? How much time should you spend on the walk through of the policy? How much time would you take for the activity? Are you sure you'll have time left over for a debrief?

The estimated time column helps make sure you've budgeted the time in your lesson plan as accurately as possible. Sure, things may come up during a session, and you may need to spend more time in one area and possibly breeze through some others, but you need a starting point. Would the lesson plan in Table 2-3 be more helpful?

Table 2-3. Estimating Time With Precision

Estimated Time	Content and Key Points	Instructional Technique
7 minutes	Introduce new policy: • Explain reasons for the changes • Locate the new policy in the handbook • Q&A	Lecture
13 minutes	Form writing activity: • Distribute materials (blank forms and copies of sample receipts) • Give participants about 10 minutes to complete the form	Individual activity

Building the Formal Learning Experience

Table 2-3. Estimating Time With Precision (Cont.)

Estimated Time	Content and Key Points	Instructional Technique
10 minutes	Debrief: • Ask for a volunteer to share how they filled out the form • Show slide with correctly filled out form • Q&A	Large group discussion

When you're building an instructor-led learning experience, it's helpful to know just how much time you have budgeted for each component and activity. Understanding how you're allocating your time will help you avoid inadvertently running out of time because you'll know what you can realistically squeeze into your session.

Content and Key Points

As you can see from the example in Table 2-4, you need not write a verbatim script when you're crafting a lesson plan for an ILT experience. However, it is helpful to identify key talking points and activity instructions.

If you were asked to deliver an ILT session and you could choose between the lesson plan segment in Table 2-4 or Table 2-5, which would you prefer to use?

Table 2-4. Outlining Content and Key Points

Estimated Time	Content and Key Points	Instructional Technique
30 minutes	Name tag switch icebreaker: • Introduce activity • Rotate groups every 4 minutes • Bring group back together to debrief after 3 rotations	Large group icebreaker activity
10 minutes	Debrief	Large group discussion

31

Chapter 2

Table 2-5. Outlining Content and Key Points With Greater Detail

Estimated Time	Content and Key Points	Instructional Technique

30 minutes	Name tag switch icebreaker:
	• Explain that you're about to do an icebreaking activity, but note that it's important for participants to listen to all instructions before standing up.
	• Ask participants to find someone in the room that they don't know and take 2 minutes to introduce themselves by answering these questions:
	  ◦ What is your name?
	  ◦ How long have you been in your role?
	  ◦ What is your hometown?
	  ◦ What is one thing you like about sales?
	• After 2 minutes, the other person should share their own answers.
	• Tell participants to begin.
	• After the first rotation, ask participants to stop where they are and to listen for a new set of instructions.
	• Tell participants:
	  ◦ Switch name tags with your partner.
	  ◦ Find a new partner.
	  ◦ When your new partner asks you these questions, give the answers from the perspective of the person whose name tag you are wearing.
		Large group icebreaker activity

	• After 4 minutes, ask participants to switch name tags again and find another new partner. • After 4 minutes, bring the attention back to the large group. • One by one, ask participants to introduce themselves according to the person whose name tag they are wearing. • After a participant shares, ask the real person to verify the responses, and then that person can introduce themselves according to their name tag. • Proceed until everyone has been introduced. • Ask participants to return to their seats.	

Building the Formal Learning Experience

Table 2-5. Outlining Content and Key Points With Greater Detail (Cont.)

Estimated Time	Content and Key Points	Instructional Technique

10 minutes	Debrief
	• Ask participants how this activity might relate to today's training on sales skills.
	• If participants don't cover these points, be sure to mention them:
	  ◦ In sales conversations, it's extremely important to listen to the person in front of you and remember key pieces of information that they're sharing.
	  ◦ Sometimes you need to be able to put yourself into the shoes of your customer.
		Large group discussion

I'm willing to put money on the fact that most of you would prefer Table 2-5. Yet Table 2-4 is what I observe many participants creating in my train-the-trainer courses. When I ask why, the responses I get include:

- "I know what I have to talk about, so I don't need to write detailed notes."
- "I don't have a lot of time."
- "It's just an outline. I'll fill in more during the actual session."

All these responses are fair, but what happens if you're sick and someone else needs to deliver the session? What happens if you need to deliver the session again in six months and can't remember how an activity is supposed to go? What happens if you get anxious in front of a group and forget a key instruction?

Creating a more detailed outline with key talking points and instructions will make your lesson plan a more useful resource both now and in the future.

Instructional Technique

The final column on this lesson plan template is a quality check. Have you varied your delivery methods enough?

If your lesson plan looks like Table 2-6, on the next page, you might want to rethink your session.

Chapter 2

Table 2-6. Attempt at Assigning Instructional Techniques to Content

Estimated Time	Content and Key Points	Instructional Technique
10 minutes	Provide an overview of our hiring process: • Need identified • Job announcement created and published • Initial review of candidates • Phone screening • Panel interview • Candidate selection • Offer • Onboarding	Lecture
5 minutes	Quickly discuss hiring manager requirements: • Meeting with human resources business partner • Setting job requirements and timeline	Lecture
15 minutes	Walk through the interview process: • Identifying qualified candidates • Ranking candidates • Creating interview questions • Reviewing interview scoring matrix • Discussing the importance of objectively evaluating candidates	Lecture

Lecture, lecture, lecture. It may be tempting to use the excuse that you're short on time or money to put together anything more varied or engaging. However, that's simply not true.

All this lesson plan accomplishes is getting your talking points out into the open. It's impossible to tell if anyone will be able to do anything new, differently, or better as a result of a session like this, even if you're the most captivating speaker in the world.

So how can you vary your techniques, keep your learners engaged, and insert an opportunity to see if your learners are getting it?

Maybe your first instinct is to throw in an activity, or perhaps you want to add a quick round of *Jeopardy* because someone suggested that games or gamification can liven up the experience. Don't listen to these instincts. Haphazardly

34

Building the Formal Learning Experience

inserting activities for the sake of switching things up isn't a good idea. Instead, there's a better option.

A 4-Step Instructional Technique Model

I've found the Anchor-Content-Application-Future Use model to be the most helpful way to ensure a training program includes a variety of instructional techniques. I was first introduced to it when I worked for the National Court Appointed Special Advocates (CASA) Association. I've searched for a source to credit this model but have not been able to find one, so I'll credit my awareness of it to National CASA.

Anchor

When it comes to instructional techniques, this is probably the one that most people forget about or don't think to include in their training. Anchor activities are designed to introduce learners to a new topic without overwhelming them with a bunch of new information from the start. For example, if you're putting together a session about a customer service model that people should be using, your learners may not find it helpful to jump right into the model. They may want to know why you're asking them to use it.

An anchor activity might be something as simple as asking people to share their worst experiences on the receiving end of poor customer service. Once you've heard a few examples, you can then share how your amazing customer service model is designed to avoid any of those customer service horror stories. Other anchor activities include:

- Tell a short story about the topic.
- Take a quick poll that revolves around your topic.
- Facilitate a guided visualization to have learners imagine what life would be like if they applied their newfound knowledge or skills.
- Play a quick round of trivia to see how much learners already know about the topic.

Content

The content step is usually when you share the bulk of the information about your topic. Often, people default to lectures, and that's fine as long as they're

35

Chapter 2

surrounded by the other three steps in this model. Other (nonlecture) content activities include:

- Offer a top 10 list of the most important things someone needs to know about your content. This could also be a top three or seven list.
- Post key concepts, definitions, facts, or figures around the room, and ask your learners to do a gallery walk to digest key information and then be prepared to talk about it.
- Show a video of an expert in the field.
- Provide a case study and ask learners to identify key concepts and how they work in a real-world context.
- Distribute an article.

Application

It will be tough to know if your learners understand the content unless they have a chance to show you. Application activities are designed to offer learners practice opportunities in a setting without real-world consequences. Returning to the customer service model example, this is when your learners can practice putting the model to use, perhaps through a role play. Other examples of application activities include:

- Create small group discussions and large group debriefs.
- Brainstorm how the concepts will work in real life and what challenges learners may need to navigate.
- Provide a form or a template for learners to complete.
- Use a checklist or rubric to evaluate work samples.

Future Use

While this fourth and final step doesn't need to occur throughout your entire lesson plan, it is a helpful step to give learners opportunities to identify how they can use their newfound knowledge or skills outside the training environment. The most traditional future use activity is an action plan, but you may also want to consider:

- Provide a self-evaluation for learners to identify their strengths and weaknesses about the topic.
- Give learners time for individual journaling or reflection.

Building the Formal Learning Experience

- Challenge learners to record a video of themselves applying their new knowledge or skill after they've left the training room, and ask them to send those videos to you for feedback.

Diversifying Your Instructional Techniques

Now that you know about the range of techniques you might want to use, let's revisit the instructional technique section of the lesson plan example (Table 2-7).

Table 2-7. Diversifying the Instructional Techniques

Estimated Time	Content and Key Points	Instructional Technique
10 minutes	Provide an overview of the hiring process.	
4 minutes	Ask participants to think of their best hiring experience (from their perspective as a job candidate). Ask several volunteers to share adjectives to describe what made those experiences so good.	Large group discussion
6 minutes	Review the steps in the hiring process: • Need identified • Job announcement created and published • Initial review of candidates • Phone screening • Panel interview • Candidate selection • Offer • Onboarding	Lecture
5 minutes	Quickly discuss hiring manager requirements.	
3 minutes	Ask participants why having a process is important.	Lecture
2 minutes	Briefly mention the hiring manager requirements: • Meeting with HRBP • Setting job requirements and timeline	Lecture

37

Chapter 2

Table 2-7. Diversifying the Instructional Techniques (Cont.)

Estimated Time	Content and Key Points	Instructional Technique
15 minutes	Walk through interview process	
8 minutes	Provide case study on a candidate going through the interview process.	Case study
7 minutes	Ask learners to identify where in the case study they found these key points: • Identifying qualified candidates • Ranking candidates • Creating interview questions • Reviewing interview scoring matrix • Objectively evaluating candidates	Large group debrief

When comparing this version to Table 2-6, you can see there are ways to get information across without relying exclusively on lectures. In fact, preparing a good lecture with clear talking points may even be more time consuming than what's laid out in the table. It doesn't take much time and you don't need to create a lot of slides when you design an activity asking people about their best previous experience being hired. When they share, they're giving you (and the rest of the class) your content while also being actively engaged!

TIME SAVER
"I Just Need Something That's Good Enough"

You may be reading this and thinking: "Yeah, adult learning is great, but seriously, I have a slide deck, and we just need to turn it into a training course. My boss is asking for it by the end of the week. In an ideal world, I'd do all this lesson planning, but I just need something that's good enough."

You may not find permission to do something like this in a lot of instructional design books, articles, or social media conversations, but I'm giving you permission. You have your content, and that's great, but don't forget to include an anchor and an application activity. Basically, your time saver formula could look like this:

Building the Formal Learning Experience

Anchor Activity	Your Content and Slides	Application Activity
• Share a famous quote or song lyric, and find a way to connect it to your topic. • Ask learners about their best or worst experience with your topic, and share how your presentation will help maximize the best experiences or minimize the worst experiences. • Use several poll questions to gauge the learners' current knowledge about your topic. • Challenge learners to share their thoughts about your topic by starting a sentence and then asking them to fill in the end. • Ask learners to think of a time when your topic could have been helpful to them. • Promise learners that your topic will solve a problem for them and explain how.		• Quiz people on the key points they should learn. • Break learners up into small groups and ask them to brainstorm how they'll use the information. • Instruct learners to complete a task or fill out a form to demonstrate they can do something with the information you've presented. • Ask learners to brainstorm potential barriers to doing something with the information and how they can overcome those barriers. • Present a case study, and ask learners to discuss what the concepts look like in an actual use case.

Keep in mind that this is a "good enough" strategy that will get content into the hands of your learners and incorporates some engaging, active learning strategies. This is also transferable to e-learning course design to engage learners in active learning practices through an anchor and application activity.

Be advised, however, that skipping over the analysis step in ADDIE and jumping right into a quick fix or good enough solution does not guarantee that people will use the information or that it was a smart idea in the first place. While I've given you permission, I highly recommend doing so only in case of emergency.

Chapter 2

Facilitator and Participant Guides

I've shared a basic lesson plan template to help you map out your thoughts. If you're the only person facilitating the training session, then you may be happy with this lesson plan. If you need a more polished set of trainer materials, you may want to move all your activity instructions and talking points into a polished document like a facilitator guide.

Note that your facilitator guide should not be a verbatim script. Different people will have different philosophies on this, but I fall firmly in the camp that thinks it's a bad idea to put a verbatim script in facilitator materials. I've seen too many instances when the facilitator—no matter how much they swore they wouldn't do this—spent the entire session looking at their notes and reading the script. For participants, this can feel like an elementary classroom's story time, except the story generally isn't as exciting.

A facilitator needs basic talking points, but they also need to be present for the group in front of them and aware of how they're responding to the information. When a facilitator is reading from a guide, they can't be fully present to the needs of their learners.

TOOL
Facilitator Guide

A more refined and polished facilitator guide should be a resource that anyone who has some basic knowledge of a topic should be able to pick up and navigate to provide effective instruction. In appendix A, you'll find a facilitator guide template that my colleagues and I have used on several projects.

Just like the facilitator needs a resource, so too will the learners, and in longer sessions, a formal participant guide may be warranted. A participant guide is a resource that assembles all learner materials in one place—case studies, articles, content, activities, job aids, and space for journaling. It's something learners can use and refer to long after the training event has wrapped up. For shorter sessions, a handout or collection of handouts may suffice. Keep in mind that you may find unique and creative inspiration to borrow from others' handouts.

Figure 2-1 is an example of a handout that my team created for a client who wanted us to train salespeople on a new service the company was offering. The

40

Building the Formal Learning Experience

salespeople were adept at selling products but uneasy about selling a service. So, we chose to design the entire learning experience around putting the idea of selling a service on trial. The learners formed the jury and would ultimately need to issue a verdict about whether selling the service would be a good idea. To set the tone, we asked all learners to walk into the classroom and read the handout on their desks (Figure 2-1).

Figure 2-1. Example Participant Handout

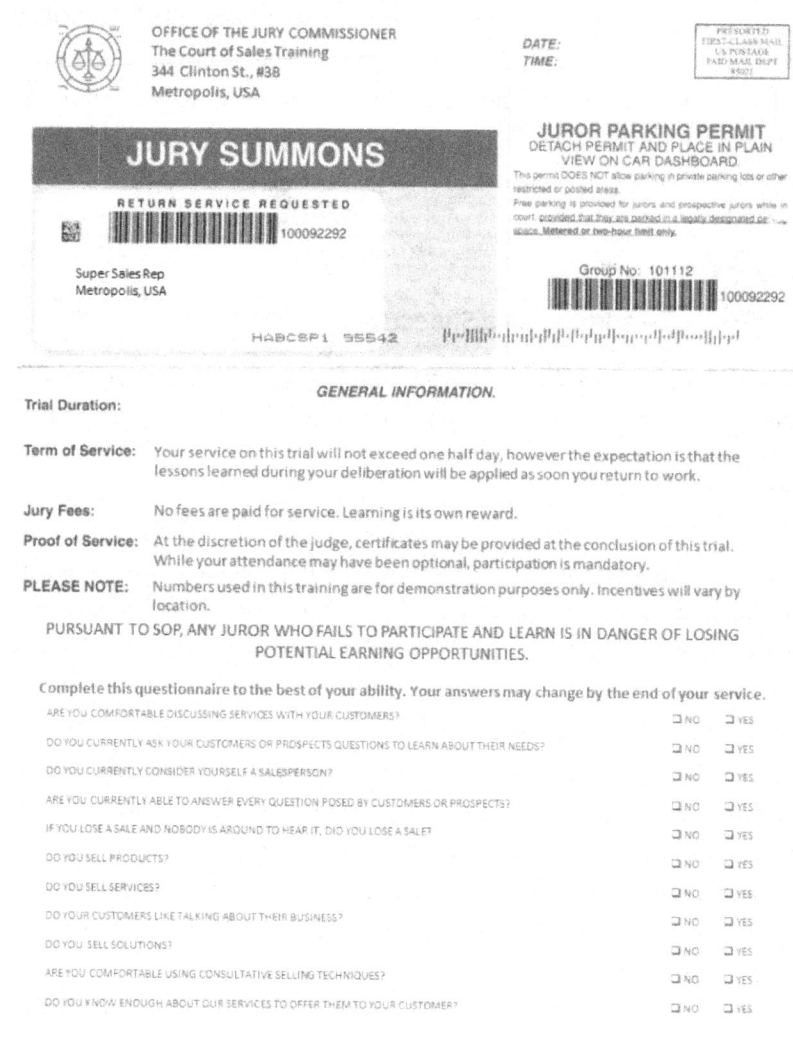

Source: *Endurance Learning. Used with permission.*

Chapter 2

The handout was a simple checklist for the first activity of the day, but it was designed as a jury summons. It helped set the tone and establish the metaphor of a trial that we'd be using for the entire training program.

Building a Learning Experience That Includes E-Learning

The other common option for formal training is e-learning.

I worked on my first e-learning project in 2007. The nonprofit I worked for paid a vendor $70,000 for the module because it needed to be coded from scratch. Today, if you need to build an e-learning module in-house (quickly and cheaply), you can use rapid authoring tools without needing to know anything about coding. (In chapter 7, you'll find a list of rapid authoring tools that are available at several price points.)

> **DEEPER DIVE**
> ### E-Learning on a Shoestring
>
> While this book will help you get started with planning and building an e-learning course, for more depth, you can turn to another book in the series: *E-Learning Design on a Shoestring*.

Even though you can build e-learning modules quickly and without paying a vendor a lot of money, it doesn't mean you should simply upload a slide deck into a rapid authoring tool and call it an e-learning course. If that's what you're planning to do, you may as well just distribute the PowerPoint slide deck.

E-learning offers you the chance to imagine what's possible. Because of its digital nature, e-learning can allow you to create real-life settings, have learners engage with avatars, and set up realistic practice scenarios that are, in my opinion, more meaningful than any in-person role play could ever be.

All of this is possible on a shoestring, as long as you have a little knowledge about instructional design, some templates to get you started, and a few examples for inspiration.

Like using a lesson plan for an ILT course, you can use a storyboard template to help you organize your thoughts for an e-learning project.

Many of the components of an e-learning storyboard are similar to components of the ILT lesson plan. That's because the foundational principles of instructional design do not change whether you're mapping out an ILT, e-learning program, or informal learning resource project. Let's explore each of the components.

TOOL
E-Learning Storyboard Template

In appendix A, you'll find an e-learning storyboard template. It can not only help keep your thoughts organized before you bring the content to life in the e-learning authoring tool, but it can also help keep everyone involved in the project (SMEs, the e-learning developer, and key stakeholders who need to review the content) on the same page. Using this storyboard to map your thoughts and get the approval of reviewers about the sequence, flow, and content prior to building your e-learning module in an authoring tool can save you both time and money on an e-learning project.

Title

Similar to the ILT program lesson plan, you can have a straightforward title (such as "Customer Service Basics") or something a little more intriguing for your learners (like "The Customer Isn't Always Right, But They Do Pay Our Bills"). The title of your courses will often depend on the workplace culture as well as your intended audience.

Objectives

This isn't a place for you to list the topics and talking points you intend to cover in the e-learning module. Learning objectives in this template should be reserved specifically for what your learner should be able to do differently or better as a result of the module. This is what will make the difference between simply adding content to your LMS that resembles a slide deck with "next" arrows to advance through the module, and a learning experience created with sound instructional design practices.

If you're trying to hasten the pace of your e-learning design and development process, then forming well-written objectives can help. If, for example,

Chapter 2

you write the following objective, who knows where your e-learning design will take you.

By the end of this module, learners will understand our sales model.

This objective is too ambiguous. Will you just share information about your sales model? Will you outline the steps? Will you ask the learners to do anything with this information during the learning experience? If not, why would they care? Why wouldn't they just click through the information so they can officially complete the course? The better written your objectives are, the easier it will be to design your e-learning module. Let's try again:

By the end of this module, learners will be able to list the four steps of our sales model.

With this objective you know that your design should include some information about the steps of your sales model and an activity challenging learners to list the steps in the correct order. This is great if you want your learners to memorize the order of the steps. Of course, if you want your learners to be able to go beyond just listing the steps, you may craft your learning objective differently. Here's one option:

By the end of this module, learners will be able to follow the steps of our sales model.

This may be more complex, but if it is the outcome that you'd like people to achieve after completing your e-learning module, then designing the appropriate e-learning activity should be your goal. Perhaps you'd design an activity that breaks up a sales conversation into four different dialogue bubbles for your learner to drag and drop into the correct order. Or you could design a branching scenario that gives the learner several ways to respond to a customer's needs, with the correct choices aligning with your sales model.

The learning objective section of your storyboard, if well written, can nudge you toward designing meaningful learning activities that increase the likelihood that your e-learning experience will yield the results you're looking for. When it comes to the meat of this storyboard, let's use a completed sample to illustrate the importance of each field (Table 2-8).

The learning objective section of your storyboard, if well written, can nudge you toward designing meaningful learning activities that increase the likelihood that your e-learning experience will yield the results you're looking for. When it comes to the meat of this storyboard, let's use a completed sample on the next page to illustrate the importance of each field (Table 2-8):

- **ID.** This column breaks your module down into screen-by-screen interactions. In the example, we used *M1_A1* and *M1_A2* for *Module 1* (M1), *first section* (A), *first screen* (1), and *Module 1* (M1), *first section* (A), *second screen* (2). You can use any coding you'd like, but it should make sense to whomever will be developing your e-learning module. Paying attention to your ID coding will allow you to match information from your storyboard with the information in your e-learning authoring tool.

- **Screen text.** This column shows exactly what text should appear on any given screen in your module. Perhaps you're the person developing the e-learning module in an authoring tool, or maybe it's someone else. This storyboard is designed to help the development phase of your e-learning project go quickly and smoothly. If you use this column to show only what should appear on screen, it can be copied and pasted right into the authoring tool.

- **Developer notes.** This column allows you to make notes to yourself (or whomever is building the e-learning module). There are times, as you build out an e-learning module, when you need to note something that is not intended to appear on the screen. In Table 2-8, this includes syncing imagery that should fade onto the screen with the voiceover file. It also includes instructions on where and when navigation should be locked. This is a very important column, and it's crucial to be as specific as possible. This is also the column where you can indicate which quiz answers are correct or incorrect and when certain feedback should pop up on the screen.

- **Voice-over.** This column is used if you add a voice-over to the e-learning module. It serves as the script that you (or a voice-over artist) will read and be inserted into a specific screen. To save time and needless confusion or frustration, each voice-over clip should be a separate audio file that's labeled and organized with the corresponding code you've entered in the ID column.

Chapter 2

Table 2-8. Completed E-Learning Storyboard Sample

ID	Screen Text	Developer Notes	Voice-Over (VO)
M1_A1	Welcome to Endurance Learning 101	Animate and fade in images of team members, one at a time, during VO. Images are found at and labeled with the order in which they should appear at drive.google.com/drive /folder/images.	Welcome to Endurance Learning 101, and welcome to the team! This brief e-learning module will give you an introduction to our company, our team, our culture, and our work. It's our hope that this module helps you better understand our organization and how your role fits in to our larger picture.
M1_A2	A tour of Endurance Learning: • Where we've been • Who we are • How we work • Your next steps	This is the menu screen and home page. Learners should return to this page after they complete each section. Initially, "Where we've been" should be the only section that is unlocked. Once learners complete the first section, the next section should be unlocked. The VO should only run the first time learners see this screen.	This module should take you approximately 20 minutes to complete, but be forewarned: You'll need to complete a challenge at the end, so don't rush through the information and activities! Feel free to take as much time as you'd like in each section. The module has been broken down into four sections: • Where we've been • Who we are • How we work • Your next steps We hope you find this module helpful as you begin your work at Endurance Learning!

Source: Endurance Learning.

Building the Formal Learning Experience

 **DEEPER DIVE**
Voice-Over, Text on Screen, or Both?

Many clients I've talked with request text on each screen and a voice-over to match. Many learners I've talked with resent being able to read the text on the screen and then having to wait for the voice-over to catch up with them. So, what's the right mix of on-screen text and voice-overs? You can explore what the research says (and then have a good response in your back pocket the next time someone asks for voice-overs and on-screen text to mimic each other) by reading the following:

- Ruth C. Clark and Richard E. Mayer, _E-Learning and the Science of Instruction: Proven Guidelines for Consumers and Designers of Multimedia Learning,_ 4th ed. (Hoboken, NJ: John Wiley and Sons, 2016).

Additional Considerations

Keep in mind that the information in this section is relatively high level—there is an entire book in the On a Shoestring series devoted to e-learning. However, because you've chosen to read this book, I want to quickly cover a few additional considerations if you choose to build an e-learning experience on a shoestring:

- **Ensure that your e-learning experience is inclusive for all potential learners.**
  - Using alternative text (sometimes called alt tags) to provide descriptions of visual imagery or objects that are picked up by screen readers can make your e-learning experience more accessible to learners with visual impairments.
  - If you're using a voice-over, adding closed captioning will be important for learners with hearing impairments.
  - Finding imagery and using names in case studies that represent the demographics of your learners can be more time consuming, but will offer your learners a better experience and make each person feel like they can see themselves in the design of your course.
- **Monitor important data.**
  - Most LMSs allow you to track basic data such as who has started a course, who has completed a course, and whether someone passed the course's final assessment.

47

Chapter 2

- If you need to track and monitor a more robust set of data, you'll want to consider using xAPI (Experience Application Programming Interface), which allows you to record, track, and monitor just about anything to do with a learner's interactions with your e-learning experience. Do you want to know how much time a learner spent on a specific screen, whether they used the help feature you spent days perfecting, or how many embedded videos they viewed? xAPI can track all this and more. You can quickly find out more about xAPI in Megan Torrance and Rob Houck's *TD at Work* issue "Making Sense of xAPI."

- **Will this e-learning experience need to be made available in other languages?** If you need to translate your e-learning experience into another language, you should keep this in mind from the beginning—it can affect many design considerations, including:

    - **Imagery.** It's easy to change on-screen text into another language, but it can be considerably more difficult if you have text in an image file. Beyond any text in imagery that may need to be translated, you'll also want to consider how well any imagery of people, offices, or backgrounds will translate for global audiences.

    - **Accessibility and alt tags.** Don't forget about any text that has been adapted for screen readers or closed captioning—it will need to be translated into other languages too.

    - **Reviewers.** Whether you are creating the original material from your own expertise or working with a SME, you will need additional reviewers who can read the translated content. Be sure to communicate expectations and timelines with translators and reviewers.

A Shoestring Summary

Building a lean, tight, coherent, on-point formal learning experience will require some ruthlessness. Eliminating superfluous information, stories, or activities that don't meet your stated learning objectives will help reduce the time (and in some instances, the costs) involved with creating a training program.

Building formal learning experiences—whether they're ILT or e-learning programs—is a process that can move quickly and inexpensively with some initial planning, so this chapter has revolved heavily around using templates to ensure high-quality instructional design.

In the next chapter, which discusses informal learning experiences, the design process can get messier because of the informal nature of the resources. That said, informal learning can also save a ton of time and money if you don't need to rely exclusively on formal or lengthy traditional experiences such as ILT and e-learning programs.

3
Building the Informal Learning Experience

There's an old saying that goes like this: "When all you have is a hammer, everything looks like a nail." When I entered the world of learning and development, I viewed every learning challenge or skill gap as a need for formal training. Whether an ILT or e-learning course, formal training was the only tool I had in my toolbox, and I was ready to bludgeon people with it for any learning need. To this day, I still need to be reminded from time to time that there are other options for learning design.

When building a learning experience on a shoestring, the absolute worst thing you can do is assume it needs to be a formal training program. Just because someone says, "We need training," doesn't mean they actually need training.

So, just like in chapter 2, I'm giving you a list of reasons to not simply default to developing a formal training program when someone comes to you and says, "We need training!"

- The target audience may not need training. They may just need to *understand* something. (People don't need training to understand something.) A job aid, handout, or checklist might work.
- Sometimes, no amount of training will solve a problem.
- Training might be *a* solution but it might not be the *best* solution.
- The target audience may already know what they should be doing, but they don't have the right motivation, incentives, or support to do it. The knowledge or skill to be taught is important yet not urgent or frequently used.

Chapter 3

- The target audience's supervisors are not supportive. (Keep in mind that if supervisors don't support or hold people accountable for putting key lessons from training into action, the likelihood of learners transferring their new knowledge or skills to the job decreases exponentially.)
- The target audience can't take time away from their job. (Think retail salespeople who are paid to work with customers or behind a cash register.)
- The skills gap or learning need is urgent and must be addressed quicker than the time it would take to create any effective formal training program.

So, before you say, "OK, I can create a training course for you!" stop and think if that's the right answer. Here are some questions that might help you save time and money that would otherwise be spent on designing and developing an unnecessary formal learning experience:

- What needs to change or be different?
- What would happen if we didn't provide training?
- How do we know that new knowledge, skills, or abilities will lead to the desired results?
- What factors beyond new knowledge, skills, or abilities could be affecting performance?
- Why now?
- Who is the target audience? (And how do we know they need training?)
- What resistance can we anticipate from the target audience (or their supervisors) if we tell them that they'll need to take this training course?
- A year from now, how will we know this training course was successful?
- Who or where would the training course content come from?

Your answers may lead you to conclude that formal training is needed, and the structure introduced in chapters 1 and 2 can help you build those programs. On the other hand, you may realize that investing time and money into building a formal training program isn't necessary. That's where this chapter comes in.

One of the best, yet least used, ways for an organization to provide instruction on a shoestring is through informal learning experiences. In terms of

Building the Informal Learning Experience

organizational learning strategy, the truth is that employees are using informal strategies on their own to learn new things all the time. They look things up on Google or YouTube, they ask colleagues for answers, and they upload resources for others to use on the intranet.

This chapter shares ideas for taking advantage of informal learning experiences in your organization—through job aids, microlearning courses, videos, stretch assignments, hands-on work, drip campaigns, and chatbots—and provides resources to stretch your budget and save people time they would normally spend in a formal learning experience.

Building a Learning Experience That Includes a Job Aid

A *job aid* is a tool or resource that someone can use to help them perform a task or remind them how to do something. It may be a standalone resource that someone can use to perform a task, even when they have no prior knowledge or experience in the area. A job aid can also be distributed as part of a formal learning experience to help people remember how to do something new, differently, or better when they leave the training environment.

There are plenty of times when formal training is an appropriate solution, but it never hurts to ask: "Do people really need to be trained on this, or will a job aid suffice?" The question is always important, but it's especially important when you're operating on a shoestring. Table 3-1 offers some example scenarios in which you may want to use a job aid, either to supplement a formal learning experience or to serve as a standalone resource.

Table 3-1. When and How to Use a Job Aid

When should you build a job aid?	What formats may be most helpful?
Listing or reminding people about steps in a process or procedure	• Bulleted list • Checklist • Document listing the steps and a short narrative describing each • Flowchart • Illustrated guide (such as Ikea's furniture assembly instructions) • Video tutorial

53

Chapter 3

Table 3-1. When and How to Use a Job Aid (Cont.)

When should you build a job aid?	What formats may be most helpful?
Offering shortcuts for using software or systems	• Cheat sheet with keystroke commands • Quick reference guide
Assessing someone's work or performance	• Rubric • Evaluation template or form
Performing calculations	• Data table
Making decisions	• Automated wizard • Flowchart or decision tree • Pros and cons list
Responding to common questions or objections	• Frequently asked questions (FAQ) document • Customer service or sales script

Building a Learning Experience That Includes Microlearning

In their book, *Microlearning: Short and Sweet*, Karl Kapp and Robin Defelice (2019) define *microlearning* as "an instructional unit that provides a short engagement in an activity intentionally designed to elicit a specific outcome from the participant."

Some people suggest that a microlearning experience can be no longer than a minute, or five minutes, or 20 minutes. The truth is that no centralized authority has been empowered to declare exactly how long something can be before it no longer counts as microlearning.

TIME SAVER
Building a Rubric

Providing feedback can be difficult for several reasons. It can be uncomfortable and subjective. Sometimes, a person believes feedback is necessary but doesn't think they have the right expertise to offer feedback of value. Someone may give better feedback with training, but if they don't have time or an opportunity for that a rubric can offer structure and an objective set of criteria for providing feedback.

A *rubric* is a guide that lists specific criteria for evaluating a behavior or performance. Here's part of a rubric for evaluating training delivery:

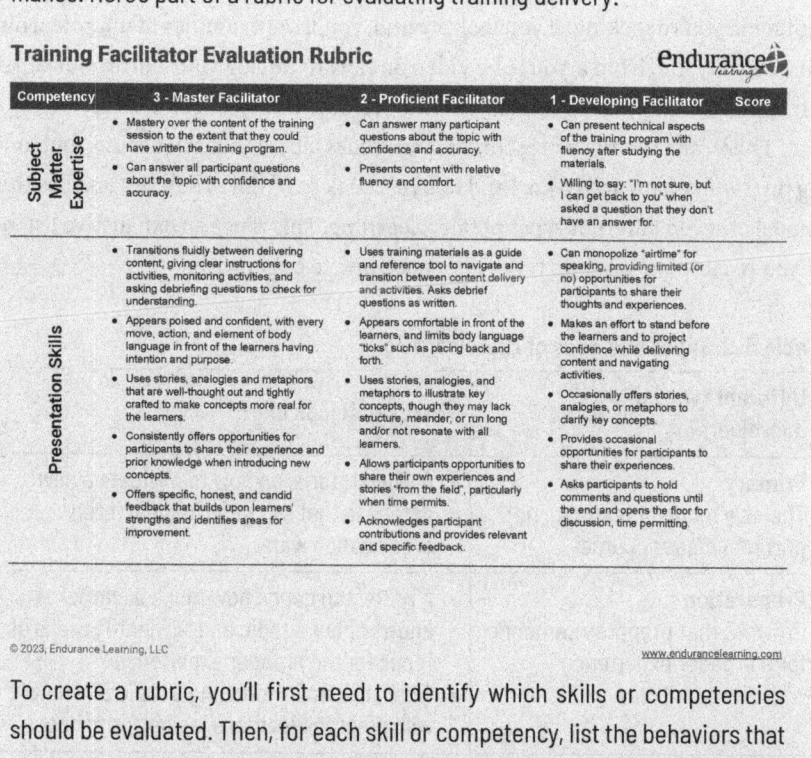

To create a rubric, you'll first need to identify which skills or competencies should be evaluated. Then, for each skill or competency, list the behaviors that should be observed if someone is performing below, at, and above expectations.

While this is not a substitute for more meaningful and complete training on evaluating performance and delivering feedback, it can offer a quick and easy way for you to provide specific, targeted, and relevant information.

In a podcast interview I did with Karl in 2022, he talked about the idea of defining microlearning by how much time it takes. When it comes to measuring microlearning by time, he said, "That's the wrong measurement. It's like measuring butts in seats. How many people did you train last year? How good was your training? Well, we trained 10,000 people last year. Is that good or not? We don't know. How was your microlearning? Oh, it's 10 minutes. Oh, OK. It totally misses the point when you make the learning timebound" (Kapp and Defelice 2022).

Chapter 3

The key thing to remember about microlearning is that it is intended to be laser focused and it should take no more time than is necessary to achieve the outcome you're seeking. If you look around, you'll see examples of microlearning in everyday life, from a YouTube video on how to unclog your bathroom sink to an app with one-minute tutorials on how to improve your golf swing.

There are plenty of resources and books about microlearning, but once again, I will offer a nod to Karl and Robyn's book as I frame Table 3-2 and use their model of seven different types of microlearning. This is not an exhaustive list, but if you're running short on time, it's a good one to begin with.

Table 3-2. Types and Uses of Microlearning

Different types of microlearning	What can it look like?
Primary The only mode of learning, not part of a bigger course	• A video tutorial on how to navigate a new database that has been implemented organization wide
Preparation Prework that prepares someone for a broader experience	• A pretest to gauge how much a learner knows about a topic and to identify areas of focus for the broader experience • A short video introducing a topic and how it will affect the learner's job performance
Post-Instruction Follow-up to a formal learning experience	• An automated post-training quiz that challenges learners to access information they learned in the course • A video (or series of videos) that goes deeper into a topic that was covered at a high level
Pensive Getting learners to think critically about a question	• A series of single-screen e-learning modules released weekly over the course of six weeks, each presenting a short case study to newly onboarded customer service agents and challenging them to identify three different ways to handle the situation

Building the Informal Learning Experience

Table 3-2. Types and Uses of Microlearning (Cont.)

Different types of microlearning	What can it look like?
Performance-Based A step-by-step look at a process or model	• A video that demonstrates what each step in a company's sales model could look like when talking with a customer • A chatbot that is connected to an organization's Slack platform and provides conversation starters and key steps for a manager or direct report in a coaching relationship when the manager types keywords into the appropriate Slack channel
Persuasive Designed to encourage you to change behaviors or attitudes	• A series of text messages to patients recovering from eye surgery, reminding them about the importance of postoperative eye drops and doctor's visits even if they think 100 percent cured • An infographic that demonstrates the impact and return on investment of a training initiative that is delivered to senior leaders who believe their training department is strictly a cost center
Practice-Based Allows the learner to receive instruction, practice a skill, and get feedback	• A language-learning app that offers instruction and then challenges the learner to speak and record practice statements in the new language (instant feedback can be given on grammar and pronunciation) • A public speaking app that is powered by artificial intelligence (AI) and asks users to speak, and then offers feedback on pauses

There is not one right way to create microlearning, but if you'd like to rethink an existing, larger course, or perhaps you have a new topic that you'd like to break down into microchunks, then the guidance that Elise Greene Margol (2017) offers in her *TD at Work* issue "Microlearning to Boost the Employee Experience" can help get you started:

- **Conduct a needs analysis.** You shouldn't cut corners on the instructional design process just because it's micro.

57

Chapter 3

- **Create sound learning objectives.** To keep your learning micro, you should limit yourself to one objective per chunk or asset. If you have more than one objective, create more than one microlearning asset and deploy a series of modules.
- **Select the right modality and delivery method.** Which medium (article, e-learning module, video, or learning game) will work best for a specific topic?
- **Incorporate it into a larger solution.** This could mean anything from organizing your microlearning chunks in an accessible resource library to including an action component for learners to demonstrate proficiency in what they've learned.

DEEPER DIVE
Microlearning

Microlearning can mean different things to different people. If you'd like a more in-depth look at what microlearning is, how it can be integrated into your learning strategy, and how to break your projects down into bite-sized, microchunks, you may want to check out these resources:

- Karl Kapp and Robin Defelice, *Microlearning: Short and Sweet* (Alexandria, VA: ATD Press, 2019).
- Elise Greene Margol, "Microlearning to Boost the Employee Experience," *TD at Work* (Alexandria, VA: ATD Press, 2017).
- Carla Torgerson and Sue Iannone, *Designing Microlearning* (Alexandria, VA: ATD Press, 2019).

Building a Learning Experience That Includes Videos

While a video can be used as a job aid or microlearning component, I want to call specific attention to this informal learning medium because it can solve many learning challenges without requiring an entire ILT or e-learning module. There are several applications for videos in learning, including:

- Introduction videos
- Explainer videos

Building the Informal Learning Experience

- Video tutorials
- Long-form videos

Some videos may run an hour or more and use professional video crews, sound equipment, and skilled actors; others may consist of co-workers having a conversation while being recorded via Zoom. Some animated videos may be high quality and created in a studio, while others may be low cost and created with affordable and easy-to-use online tools.

Sometimes people shy away from video creation because they think it will be prohibitively expensive or they need to be skilled in editing and visual design. I've worked on video projects that cost tens of thousands of dollars, and I've worked on video projects that simply cost a few hours of my time. (And trust me, I am not savvy with even simple editing software!)

During the early days of the COVID-19 pandemic, I was approached by a client who needed to convert an in-person leadership development program into a hybrid program that included live webinar sessions and asynchronous learning activities. The client desperately wanted to keep as much human connection in the program as possible, even if people couldn't participate in-person. My colleague, Tim, suggested that we still allow people from different departments to share their stories by setting up a series of Zoom calls and recording the department representatives. However, we also wanted to keep these videos short. When this leadership program met in-person, department representatives would lecture for 30 to 60 minutes, but we knew program attendees would not want to watch a monologue video that long. To make sure these videos would effectively use everyone's time, we worked with the client to identify each department representative's learning objectives, and then worked with the representatives to craft talking points, rhetorical devices, and activities they could use during their five-to-10-minute video recordings. While we needed to film several takes and edit the videos, this low-cost video strategy (combined with a series of live webinars for Q&A and other interactive pieces) allowed continuity between the in-person experience and the new, hybrid (but completely virtual) experience.

As an instructional designer, you'll need to understand the intent behind using a video as part (or all) of the learning experience, as well as how much the quality of the video production matters. If you're creating a learning experience for an external audience, you may need the video to look more professional. If

59

Chapter 3

the video is a learning tool for internal audiences, you may have more leeway on the quality of your final product.

Table 3-3 offers you a quick look at situations when you might want to use a video as part of your instructional design and some thoughts on how you might create the video.

Table 3-3. When to Use Different Types of Videos and How to Create Them

Video Type	Use Case Examples	How to Create the Video
Introduction videos	• A welcome message from the CEO as part of new employee orientation • A senior leader explaining the importance of a new initiative being launched	• Recording feature in a virtual meeting platform • Inexpensive video recording equipment and online editing software • Professional film crew
Explainer videos	• A narrated or illustrated description of how the organization generates revenue • A presurgery informational message about the risks associated with anesthesia • An introduction for new managers about annual performance review tasks and benchmarks	• Inexpensive video recording equipment and online editing software • Online animated video creation software • Recording feature on PowerPoint or other slide presentation software • Professionally created animated video
Video tutorials	• How to create pivot tables in spreadsheet software • How to navigate a specific software program • A step-by-step guide to changing a tire	• User-generated videos • Screen recording software • Recording feature on PowerPoint or other slide presentation • Inexpensive video recording equipment and online editing software
Long-form videos	• An in-depth look at a process or technical skill • A panel discussion offering a variety of viewpoints on a topic	• Inexpensive video recording equipment and online editing software • Professional film crew (possibly with paid actors)

 **DEEPER DIVE**
Building Videos for Learning

There are so many different types of videos to create for learning purposes. If you'd like more information about how to create videos for your own learning solutions, you may be interested in these videos about videos:

- Ajay Jain, "5 Key Principles for Designing and Delivering Video-Based Learning," ATD webinar, April 6, 2021, webcasts.td.org/webinar/4025.
- Matt Pierce, "Your Year for Video! Getting Started, Leveling Up, and Making Better Videos," the Visual Lounge, video, January 13, 2022, youtube.com/watch?v=QQi6NdW1P_A.

Building a Learning Experience That Includes a Stretch Assignment or Hands-On Work

If you're familiar with the 70-20-10 framework, then you're aware of the importance of stretch assignments and hands-on work for professional development. According to the Center for Creative Leadership (2022), "the 70-20-10 rule reveals that individuals tend to learn 70 percent of their knowledge from challenging experiences and assignments, 20 percent from developmental relationships, and 10 percent from coursework and training."

Any time nice round numbers (like 70, 20, and 10) are tied to a particular model or framework, you should always raise an eyebrow. On the other hand, I've never heard anyone claim to have actual data supporting the idea that every person gets exactly 70 percent of their learning from challenging assignments, 20 percent from developmental relationships, and 10 percent from formal training experiences. Therefore, the 70-20-10 framework is a valuable guideline for creating a learning strategy. If someone spends significantly more than 10 percent of their time in formal learning experiences, when are they doing their job? When creating training programs, you should not expect all learning to happen separate from an employee's daily tasks and responsibilities. So, how can instructional designers bake learning into an organization's flow of work?

Stretch assignments are assignments or tasks that go beyond a person's typical duties, which allows them to develop new knowledge, skills, or abilities. A person may have some of the knowledge or skills to take on the assignment, but

Chapter 3

perhaps they don't have all the experience that someone who usually completes the assignment has. Typically, an employee's supervisor has the responsibility to assign stretch assignments.

So, why is a book about instructional design covering an activity that happens outside the confines of a formal training program? Remember, when someone comes to you and says, "We need training!" you might not need to invest time or resources into creating a training program. You may be able to talk through the benefits of implementing stretch assignments into everyday management practices across your organization. However, not all supervisors are experienced with stretch assignments or know how to support them, so it's not helpful to tell someone, "We don't need formal training. Just throw some stretch assignments at your employees, and they'll be able to grow their skill set in no time!" Keep in mind that people doing stretch assignments intended to help build knowledge, skills, or abilities also need support. Throwing someone into an unfamiliar situation and expecting them to sink or swim is certainly one strategy, but perhaps it's not the most effective form of professional development.

As part of my first job after college, the CEO asked me to lead the negotiation of a new lease for the company's office space, which involved expanding into an adjoining office space as well as an accompanying build-out of the space and purchase of new office furniture. I was a recent college graduate with a degree in political science and had been working as the office manager for about six months when I was given this assignment. I had never negotiated anything, spoken with an architect, or seen a blueprint, and while I had worked in cubicles before, I didn't know anything about the work that went into purchasing new office furniture or equipment.

I think the CEO saw leadership potential in me and this was his way of demonstrating confidence in my ability to take on a major initiative. I also think he quickly noticed my panicked look after a round or two of negotiations. So, he paired me with a more experienced colleague who could take the lead. After months of back-and-forth conversations, a lease was signed, construction was completed, new furniture was set up, and we moved into the new space. Being paired with a more experienced colleague to coach and mentor me through the process was a godsend. Without his support, I may have still been trying to negotiate that lease today, 25 years later!

Building the Informal Learning Experience

While not all stretch assignments will be this hefty, people assigned to new projects with unfamiliar responsibilities may still require, some support from a supervisor, mentor, coach, job aid, or cohort going through similar experiences. Table 3-4 can serve as a job aid managers across your organization can use to help identify and support the most appropriate stretch assignments for their staff.

Table 3-4. Examples and Best Practices for Stretch Assignments

Stretch Assignments	For Best Results
Deliver a presentation to key stakeholders.	• Provide coaching and feedback on presentation outline. • Debrief the employee following their presentation to identify lessons learned and what to keep or adjust next time.
Lead the implementation of a new initiative.	• Provide coaching and feedback on the implementation plan • Schedule regular check-ins to discuss the success of the initiative and any obstacles.
Supervise interns or contract workers.	• Offer tools or resources on best practices for supervisors. • Schedule regular check-ins to discuss lessons learned, successes, and struggles when supervising someone.
Spearhead the communication for a new campaign.	• Provide coaching and feedback on the communication plan. • Provide example communication plans, including templates, checklists, or timelines others have used.
Lead the search for a new team member or employee.	• Review hiring policies and practices to ensure compliance with HR protocols. • Assign a more experienced person to serve as a sounding board before a final decision is made.
Organize a task force to solve an intractable business problem.	• Offer suggestions on where to find task force members as well as what qualities to look for. • Provide meeting agenda templates to ensure meetings are productive and focused. • Provide coaching and feedback on potential solution ideas.

63

Chapter 3

Table 3-4. Examples and Best Practices for Stretch Assignments (Cont.)

Stretch Assignments	For Best Results
Represent the team on a cross-functional committee.	• Set goals and expectations for their role. • Schedule regular check-ins on work or committee decisions.
Plan and facilitate a team meeting.	• Provide agenda templates to ensure meetings are productive and focused. • Debrief the employee following the meeting to discuss what worked well and what could be strengthened.
Delegate a task to a direct report.	• Provide coaching and feedback on why delegation is essential and how to identify which tasks or responsibilities to delegate.
Cover tasks for a colleague who is on vacation or long-term leave.	• Provide expectations for the work and identify what could potentially come up in the colleague's absence. • Debrief the employee after their colleague returns to discuss how effectively tasks were covered.

Building a Learning Experience That Includes a Drip Campaign

When someone is running for mayor of your town, they will tell you about their platform and why you should vote for them, but they'll never ask you to attend a half-day training session or require you to complete a 30-minute e-learning module on how to vote or why you should vote for them. So, how do you learn about different mayoral candidates?

It may begin with a lawn sign that you pass on your way home. You may receive a flier in the mail or a phone call from a supporter of the candidate. Maybe you see an internet ad or receive an email. As the election nears, you'll likely see commercials. Someone may even knock on your door. Whether you like it or not, you may begin to know the candidate's name, their slogan, and a few things they claim to be fighting for.

A so-called "drip campaign" for professional development—providing small learning resources or educational opportunities over time—adopts the same philosophy, although it should be less annoying for your target audience.

Building the Informal Learning Experience

Offering information, and then repeating it over time, has been documented to have several learning benefits. In the report *Spacing Learning Events Over Time: What the Research Says*, Will Thalheimer (2006) asserts that "Spacing repetitions over time facilitates long-term remembering. It enables our learners to store information more resistant to forgetting than non-spaced repetitions."

DEEPER DIVE

Combatting the Forgetting Curve Through Spaced Repetition

If you want your learners to use what you've taught them, they first need to remember it. The research around spaced repetition argues that learning needs to be a process, not an event. If you'd like more information about the effectiveness of spaced repetition, including research from multiple industries, then these resources may interest you:

- Will Thalheimer, *Spacing Learning Events Over Time: What the Research Says* (Somerville, MA: Work-Learning Research, 2006).
- Peter C. Brown, Henry L. Roediger III, and Mark A. McDaniel, *Make It Stick: The Science of Successful Learning* (Boston, MA: Harvard University Press, 2014).

A drip campaign brings small pieces of content about your topic to a learner over an extended period of time. One of the more common ways to do this is to send a regular cadence of emails to your intended audience. A drip campaign can include these learning artifacts:

- Articles
- Podcasts
- Videos
- E-learning modules
- Research reports (or executive summaries)
- Job aids

My organization once worked with a client to develop a new manager training program. They didn't have a big budget, but they wanted to get the best bang for their buck. As we went through the analysis and design phases of the ADDIE model, we learned that they planned to offer this training program only once. We were concerned that a one-and-done approach would not be effective

65

Chapter 3

(and that we'd be blamed for charging them money for an ineffective training program), so we approached the client with an idea that they'd never heard of before, but intrigued them immediately: What if we designed a series of learning boosts that could be deployed in a drip campaign in the weeks following the training program?

We suggested a low-cost way to automate the drip campaign, such as using a service like MailChimp to schedule emails on a regular cadence, but the client told us that they had an in-house system they could use instead. We identified articles, videos, and resources they could send—one item a week. Some of these artifacts were reminders of the content they'd learned in their session, some went deeper on a particular topic, and others introduced new content that we couldn't fit into the original training program. The client was thrilled that we could keep the duration of the initial training event short without sacrificing key information and resources, which could be slowly uncovered after the program while keeping the content top of mind for the managers.

Building a Learning Experience That Includes Chatbots and AI Technology

By now I'm sure you understand my point: A lot of informal learning opportunities are designed to provide information or help improve knowledge and skills in the moment of need. If you've ever used the chat feature on your cable company's customer service site to find self-service answers to a question about your bill, then you're familiar with *chatbots*, which are automated features that provide answers or information when you type keywords—kind of like an automated, all-knowing assistant. Recent advances in AI (machines that learn from experience and make adjustments to perform tasks) include large language models (LLMs), which have have been trained on large quantities of data and can understand and generate text, such as the AI chatbot ChatGPT.

Some organizations may have the resources to replicate an AI chatbot that integrates voice activation technology, similar to the voice assistant on your smartphone. However, when you're working on a shoestring, this funding or technology may not be available. There are many free or low-cost online tools that you can use to build a standalone chatbot, or you can integrate chatbot features into platforms your organization is already using, such as Slack.

Building the Informal Learning Experience

When using a simple chatbot, you type in a question (or keyword) and it offers you an answer (or key information). Some possible instances when a chatbot may help with a learning program (or eliminate the need for a learning program altogether) include:

- Serving as an on-demand FAQ when a new policy or program is rolled out
- Helping customer service agents quickly come up with a response to common questions
- Acting as a decision tree or troubleshooting guide
- Providing sales representatives with key product information when talking with a customer
- Helping employees determine who to contact in HR when they have questions about benefits

AI models like LLMs have only recently become available as cheap (or free) resources with user-friendly interfaces. These simple-yet-powerful tools elevate chatbots to a new level—you don't need to input any data or answers yourself because it's been done for you. They're trained on an enormous data set and have been used for everything from writing college-level essays (with references!) to passing the LSAT exam for admission into law school. Table 3-5 offers some ways that using LLMs across your organization can reduce or eliminate the need for training or formal learning programs.

Table 3-5. Uses for AI or LLMs

AI or LLMs can . . .	So you don't need to train people to . . .
Develop a complete, engaging lesson plan.	Create engaging training with activities intended to engage learners.
Provide HTML code.	Code to develop a simple website or make basic changes to an existing site.
Provide feedback on a business email.	Write basic business emails.
Instruct someone on how to create a pivot table in Excel.	Navigate and use basic spreadsheet applications.

There are several things to remember when using AI tools or LLMs. First, never enter proprietary or confidential information into them. Second, even

Chapter 3

though they've been trained on large swaths of data, these tools can still yield erroneous results. Anyone using them will still need to check the accuracy of what they generate. Third, the results may not be as inclusive of all experiences, races, ethnicities, or genders. Just because a computer produced something, doesn't mean that it is free of bias.

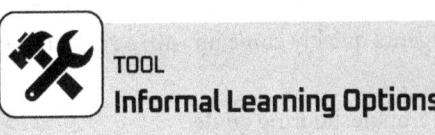

TOOL
Informal Learning Options

If you see a learning need that can be addressed without requiring people to take time away from their work to attend a training session or complete an e-learning course, then perhaps an informal learning experience (or a combination of several) may be a better option. In appendix A, you'll find some informal learning options to help you brainstorm possible solutions.

A Shoestring Summary

Remember that building a learning experience doesn't mean it needs to be a formal learning experience. Organizations can save time and money by asking whether a resource such as a job aid, video, stretch assignment, or chatbot could meet the individual's or organization's learning needs. Even if informal experiences alone won't completely meet the learning needs, they can reduce the amount of time and money spent on developing formal learning experiences.

Although technology is often used to create some informal learning experiences, it doesn't mean that building them will be expensive. There are a many tools and strategies to design, develop, and deploy informal learning experiences and they're all available at different price points.

4
Building the Learning Ecosystem

When I first started working in training and development, I was so excited about the opportunity to use creative approaches to help people learn. People would come up to me long after a training session and say, "I truly enjoyed that session you did for us. I think it might have been one of the best sessions I've ever attended!" Comments like this made me feel great. However, I found the responses to my follow-up question deflating. I'd say, "That's great to hear! What kinds of things have changed for you since that training session?" And then there would be an awkward pause, as if they were thinking, "What's with the follow-up question? Can't this guy just take the compliment and say, 'Thank you'?"

Except I couldn't just say, "Thank you." First, I'm a professional facilitator, so debriefing and follow-up questions pop out of my mouth. (Yes, I'm fun at family gatherings and parties!) Second, and more relevant to this book, training should be about behavior change and results, not whether someone enjoyed the experience. It's true that I don't want to churn out training experiences that people don't like, but just because they had fun, it doesn't mean they learned something new.

After having several of these conversations, I began to ask myself, "What makes a training program effective?" A few years later, I stumbled upon an answer to this question as I studied for my master's degree in organization development. (Note: There is no single answer, but there are some very important factors that go into it.) I was introduced to the idea of systems thinking.

There are entire books, courses, and programs devoted to systems thinking, but in short, *systems thinking* in instructional design means that people don't

69

Chapter 4

learn, develop, or do their jobs in isolation. People carry out their individual responsibilities within a larger system.

Think about the human body. You could say that it's a collection of cells, but that would be oversimplified. Some cells make up the nose, some make up the mouth, some make up the windpipe, and some make up the lungs, but when you put them all together, you have (most of) the respiratory system. When you combine the respiratory system with the digestive system, the skeletal system, and many other systems, you have the human body. If there is a problem with a few cells in one system, then you may have problems with how the other systems work. If you maintain a healthy diet, you can strengthen many of the systems. If you get blisters on your feet and they affect how you walk, you may end up with back problems. Everything is connected!

Like each part of the human body, individuals who work within an organization are connected. If one person goes through the best learning experience of their life, it doesn't mean that it will have an impact. This is a very important lesson for instructional designers.

Remember, instructional design isn't only about the design of a training session or e-learning module (which was the focus of chapter 2). Instructional design also isn't simply saying, "We don't need formal training for this, but maybe a checklist will be helpful to reduce errors" (which was the focus of chapter 3). Effective and successful instructional design takes a village.

This chapter will explore some relationships that you will need to build to create a learning initiative that has the best chance to succeed.

Building Buy-In for a Learning Program

A learning initiative is about change—individual or organizational. Can someone do something new, differently, or better to improve their impact or their organization's key metrics? Accordingly, instructional designers should also be familiar with the change management discipline.

If you Google "change management," you'll find many theories and models, but one I've seen resonate most often is John Kotter's eight-step process for leading change. While all eight steps are important (in fact, he says that the biggest reason change efforts fail is because not all eight steps are followed; Kotter 1995), the step that is essential for instructional designers to build buy-in for their learning initiatives is the first step: Establish a sense of urgency.

 DEEPER DIVE
Change Management

John Kotter developed one of the most well-known change management models based upon his work on hundreds of change projects with different organizations. He's written many books about the topic; I'll suggest two because each one caters to a different type of reader.

There are many business reasons to incorporate change management strategies into your learning initiative. This book incorporates humanity into change management as well:

- John P. Kotter and Dan S. Cohen, *The Heart of Change: Real-life Stories of How People Change Their Organizations* (Boston, MA: Harvard Business Review Press, 2002).

This second recommendation is more like a fable than a business book (but Kotter will still walk you through each of the eight steps of his change model):

- John Kotter and Holger Rathgeber, *Our Iceberg Is Melting: Changing and Succeeding Under Any Conditions* (New York: St. Martin's Press, 2006).

Think about it. If you're relaxing, sitting on the couch, watching your favorite show or sporting event, or reading a book, which of these statements would motivate you to quickly get out of the house?

- Please get out of the house now because I said so.
- Please get out of the house now because mom and dad said so.
- Please get out of the house now because it's the right thing to do.
- Please get out of the house now because a new couch is being delivered in two weeks.
- Please get out of the house now because the house is on fire and you'll burn to death if you sit there.

I hope the last statement is the most motivating. Now, think about the reasons you give to people for why they should spend time going through your learning initiatives. Do you say, "Because I said so," or "because the CEO (or HR) said so," or "because you may at some point eventually need to use this computer system." These are not arguments that will lead people to want to

Chapter 4

complete a training program. However, "Your annual bonus requires you to hit a 75 percent customer service metric, and you're currently at 62 percent" clearly states the benefit of a specific professional development initiative.

For training initiatives to succeed, you need broad support—from learners, from the learners' supervisors, and from anyone you have to petition for funding to develop the learning. To get that support, you need to think about what creating a sense of urgency might mean, and it can be different things for different people. Table 4-1 offers some ideas on how to establish a sense of urgency for several key audiences.

Table 4-1. How to Gain Buy-In From Different Stakeholders

Stakeholder	Ideas for Creating a Sense of Urgency
Learners	• Provide a clear answer to the question "What's in it for me?" • Use learning objectives that go beyond knowing or understanding, and frame them in a way that outlines how new knowledge or skills will be used to solve an immediate need or problem. • Communicate the intended benefits of the learning program in advance of a learner completing an in-person or online course. • Offer specific examples of how using the job aid or other informal resource can deliver answers to questions without leaders needing to sign up for a course or ask someone for help.
Learners' supervisors	• Provide a clear answer to the question "Why are employees taking time away from their jobs to complete this training?" (ideally using metrics). • Offer quick and easy ways for the supervisor to support their employees after the training program (such as a goal-setting form prior to the learning experience or a checklist of topics to discuss after the learning experience).
Budgetary stakeholders	• Compare the current state (ideally using metrics) with the envisioned future state (using projected metrics). • Provide evidence about how similar initiatives have been beneficial in the past. • Provide industry or scholarly data on how effective learning programs yield results.

Building the Learning Ecosystem

Building Human Connections

We don't live in a world in which our behaviors and everyone else's reactions adhere neatly to the way theories and models appear in textbooks. We can follow the principles of effective instructional design and combine them with the most effective change management models, yet our initiatives may struggle—particularly if we don't spend enough time making human connections and building relationships.

Several years ago, I was hired to lead training initiatives for one specific part of an organization—an eye bank (as in, cornea transplants)—and most employees were involved in technical processes. Existing organizational training programs had been created by technical experts, and there was no arguing with the success of their initiatives, as the organization had become one of the largest eye banks in the world, helping to restore sight to thousands of people each year.

I was the first person with an instructional design background to be hired full time by the organization. While my team was willing to immediately embrace some of the new learning design concepts and principles I introduced to them, I believed that I could help the larger organization. Unfortunately for me, leaders from other teams across the organization were too busy curing blindness to grant me time to make the case that their current training programs could be even better.

Perhaps you're thinking: "But Brian, haven't you been paying attention to this book? It should be easy enough. Just create a sense of urgency like John Kotter says!" Honestly, no amount of urgency would get teams across the organization to buy in to using a lesson plan when my co-workers were working to eliminate blindness. However, when I got away from the theory for a moment, a funny thing happened. I was working with Jen, a SME from another team in the organization, who was delivering a virtual session to a group of people my team was working with. I helped take Jen's expertise and translate it into an engaging lesson plan. After she delivered it, we went back to our respective teams, and I didn't think much more about the project.

A few days later, Jen asked if I could help with another training project she was working on. A few weeks later, another team's director told me that Jen suggested I might be able to help make their training program more engaging and less reliant on lectures and slides.

73

Chapter 4

When Brian (the trainer) tried preaching from the gospel of instructional design, my colleagues across the organization were polite, but too busy to change the way they designed training programs. But when Jen, the operations team lead—and one of their own—suggested that there might be value in changing how training programs were designed and delivered, they listened.

You do not need to be solely responsible for creating a sense of urgency. Never underestimate the power of having strong relationships across your organization to help establish buy-in for your training programs.

Building a Team to Test the Learning Program

While gaining buy-in for your instructional design projects might revolve heavily around the analysis step of the ADDIE model, building the right team for testing your learning initiative draws upon your work in the remaining steps, so you'll want to think carefully about who you choose for designing, developing, implementing, and evaluating your initiative. Keep in mind that testing your learning program shouldn't wait until you've almost completely built it out.

Design

During the design phase, when you're creating lesson plans or storyboards, it's essential that your SMEs are reviewing the work and finding any incorrect, missing, or superfluous content. They may have handed you plenty of good source material, but if you've drafted case studies or activities that are flawed, the design phase—when lesson plans or storyboards are in draft form—is the best, fastest, and least expensive time to make corrections. Waiting until later in the process could mean redoing or rebuilding significant amounts of work, and that can be a budget and project timeline killer.

If you're translating the project into other languages, this is also a good time to provide at least a sample of your content to the translator to ensure the accuracy of any technical terms. This process could require some coordination between you, the translator, and a learner who is a native speaker of the translated language. If the translator is not familiar with the subject matter, some alignment could be necessary between how words, terms, and acronyms are translated and how they are used in the content.

Development

During the development phase, quality control becomes a significant factor. For instructor-led training, you may be the person responsible for quality control—ensuring that all the activities work the way you'd imagined. When I create new activities, I'll often grab a few colleagues and schedule a "play date" to run through them to make sure that it works. The more complex your instructions, the more important this becomes. There are few things worse in the training experience than to be a learner who is receiving confusing instructions.

Not only is it important to test activities with colleagues to make sure the instructions are clear and the activities work, but it can also be important to run activities by key stakeholders or SMEs to ensure buy-in. I once suggested that my team use Play-Doh with a very experienced group of salespeople, and I initially received a lot of pushback from key stakeholders who thought it would be too elementary, and even insulting, to the target audience. However, once we tested the exercise, the SMEs and other key stakeholders turned into the biggest, most invaluable advocates for this program. The experience was such an eye-opener that the stakeholders told us there was no way they could make us change that activity. We were extremely glad we tested it and got their support before moving on.

If you're creating an e-learning module, quality assurance means that all your buttons work, your voice-over syncs with what people are seeing on their screen, and the text has been edited for grammar and spelling. The quickest way to have people leave an e-learning module (perhaps never to return again) is to release it with broken navigation.

The development phase is also when you may need to involve someone from the marketing or branding team to be sure fonts, colors, templates, and logos are consistent with what the organization allows. Just as instructional designers believe that learning objectives and measurable outcomes are the most important thing, the people whose job it is to defend the integrity and image of the organization will believe that fonts, colors, and logos are the most important.

Implementation

Depending on how big and important your learning initiative is, you may want to have several implementation stages. A pilot (or beta test) phase is when you

Chapter 4

assemble an intentionally targeted group of learners to go through the world premiere of your training program, make critical adjustments based on that experience, and then release it to the masses with a broader implementation.

Conducting a pilot program is different than bringing a few colleagues together to test activities, instructions, or functionality. With a pilot group, you go through the learning program from start to finish. For instructor-led training programs, you observe what's working and what needs tightening (or what needs to be overhauled), and you also conduct a postsession focus-group conversation. With e-learning programs, you track the user metrics and ask learners to complete a more detailed survey of their experiences—what their key takeaways were, where they may have gotten stuck, what worked for them, and what was confusing.

Even with a tight timeline, if your project is big and important enough, you'll want to use a pilot or beta test, and then refine the program based upon observations and feedback prior to the official, large-scale implementation.

Evaluation

Even with all these checkpoints, there will still be some additional stakeholders to consider when evaluating your project. Some evaluation metrics and data will be easier than others to collect. You may be able to find data on the number of people trained, pre- and post-test results, or e-learning course completion on your own (or you may need an LMS administrator's help). Other evaluation measures will require some assistance from:

- **Learners.** Post-training evaluation data can be collected at the end of the learning experience, but you shouldn't limit learner evaluation aspirations to Level 1 feedback. You may also want to consider reaching out to participants several months after they completed your course to learn more about how they're applying the new knowledge or skills on the job or if they feel more confident.
- **Learners' supervisors.** Having the learners self-report information can offer one data point, but being able to compare that data with how supervisors think their performance has (or has not) improved may offer a more objective data point.

Building the Learning Ecosystem

- **Other sources.** If other performance data—either for the individual or the organization—is available, find it and use it. This can help you document the impact of your current initiative and, if the data demonstrates good results, be used to justify future project funding. You may want to seek data that compares the sales performance of people who have taken the training course with those who haven't, data that demonstrates a reduction in waste or a reduction in on-the-job injuries following the training course, or data that demonstrates higher net promoter scores after people have completed customer service training. You'll have outlined what data you need during the analysis phase. Keep in mind that performance data also has limitations—while you can often find data that shows a correlation between training and results, it's much harder to prove a causal link between training and a shift in metrics.

Use Table 4-2 as a guide for which stakeholders to involve at different stages when creating formal or informal learning experiences.

Table 4-2. When to Involve Which Stakeholders in the Build

Phase	Stakeholders to Consider Involving
Design	• Subject matter experts • Translators (if necessary) • Learners who are native speakers of the language the content will be translated into (if necessary) • Influential stakeholders who need to buy in to (and eventually serve as advocates for) activities
Development	• Colleagues who can help test instructions and activities • Quality assurance staff (if available) • Marketing or branding representatives
Implementation	• Pilot or beta test group
Evaluation	• LMS administrator • Learners • Learners' supervisors • System administrators responsible for employee and organizational performance metrics

Chapter 4

Building Support for the Learning Program

Because learning doesn't happen in a vacuum, better performance often depends on more than instructional design alone. Before I bring this chapter to a close, I want to discuss seven common barriers that prevent a training program from being effective and some common practices to increase the likelihood that it will succeed.

TOOL

Increasing the Potential for Success

This chapter revolves around building relationships and establishing an ecosystem that will support your learning design. Use the worksheet in appendix A to identify potential barriers to your program's success and how you may address each one.

Learners Don't Think They Have Time

A few years ago, when a friend of mine who was a senior leader at a huge, Seattle-based online retailer met me for coffee, he was as excited as I'd ever seen him. He wanted to tell me about a leadership development program he'd been participating in. The program itself sounded amazing, but I was struck by the level of support he'd received from his own boss—who emailed the rest of the team to let them know my friend would not be available, should not be bothered, and would not respond to emails while he was participating in this leadership development course.

Not all learners will have such supportive supervisors, but there are some measures you might be able to take to help learners participate in your learning program without distractions and guilt. Many learners will respond to emails during an in-person session, multi-task during a virtual session, or even walk away from an e-learning module for an extended period of time.

Here are a few ways you can help prevent that from happening:

- Set clear expectations for participants they know how long the learning experience will take.
- Ask learners to block off time on their work calendars so that others can see when they're unavailable (this is particularly important, yet

Building the Learning Ecosystem

not as intuitive when learners are working on self-paced e-learning modules).

- Ask learners to make sure they are aligned with their supervisors' expectations while they are trying to improve their knowledge or skill set.

I've spoken with so many people who feel guilty that they're not doing their daily jobs while they're supposed to be learning. However, I've also spoken with many supervisors who don't have a problem if a learner isn't immediately responding to emails or working on deliverables while they're in a training session. If learners clarify with their supervisors that they have permission to be wholly present in their professional development program, their need to multitask might dissipate.

Learners Revert to Old Habits

Anyone who has ever tried going on a diet or joining a gym knows that long-term, sustainable behavior change can be difficult. Even when we know there may be a better way to do something, old habits die hard.

There are a few ways to address this challenge:

- If you're confronting an accountability issue, designing ways for learners to stay in touch, connect with other learners, and talk about ways they've applied key learning concepts can allow them to help one another.
- Make sure the learners' supervisors are involved. (I'll go deeper into this challenge later in this chapter.)
- Ask learners to report how they've implemented key elements from the training session. This strategy can be supported through offering incentives or other rewards. I've also seen it work effectively by withholding the training certificate of completion until learners follow up with the training team on how they've applied key learning concepts.

Learners Forget What They Learned

No matter how important you think your learning program is, participants can't remember everything they've been taught, no matter how engaging your instructional design. (Of course, they'll forget more information faster if it's poorly designed!)

Chapter 4

Chapter 3 was devoted exclusively to informal learning components, and several of them can help combat this challenge. Provide resources such as flowcharts, quick reference guides, cheat sheets, checklists, or rubrics during the learning experience as handouts (for instructor-led programs) or downloads (for e-learning programs). Sending follow-up information or using learning boosts after a training event can help keep your information front of mind for longer periods of time.

TIME SAVER
Standard Follow-Up Items

Sharing resources at regular intervals following the completion of a training session or e-learning module can help combat the forgetting curve and keep the topic front of mind for your learners. It's not always easy to come up with ideas for meaningful follow-up items, so use this list to get started:

- An article that goes deeper on the topic
- A checklist of action items the learner can or should be taking to practice their new knowledge, skills, or abilities
- A video (either an internal resource or a credible clip from YouTube)
- A handout summarizing key points from the learning event
- A question of the day (or week) quiz question about your content

Learners Don't Know How to Apply What They've Learned

Think about sitting through a training course that focuses on the important elements of a courageous conversation related to diversity, equity, and inclusion. You've learned about the elements of courageous conversations. You've been convinced that even though they may be uncomfortable, they're important. You've spent time in a small group discussing a case study and dissecting what someone did well and what someone should have done differently.

Three days later, you hear a colleague tell a joke that you're sure would offend a lot of people. Your heart begins to race. It's time. You were just in that training course, and you think you should say something. You open your mouth . . . then you close it.

80

Building the Learning Ecosystem

You don't know where to begin. You may have left the training course with the ability to explain the value of a courageous conversation and identify the strengths and weaknesses of one, but you never actually practiced how to have one.

This dilemma isn't just about courageous conversations. It's about having sales conversations, engaging employees in coaching, handling customer complaints, and performing technical tasks. When a learner hasn't been given the opportunity to practice in a comfortable environment without consequences (such as role playing or other practice scenarios to learn from feedback), it will be more difficult for them to know what to do on the job. Your learning objectives matter, and so does your learners' time—it's much more valuable to spend time helping them practice how to do new things, even if they protest when you knowingly grin and say, "OK, now it's time to role play."

Learners Don't Have Access to Technology or Resources

If you're putting together a training program to increase user adoption of a computer system, it's important to ensure the learners will have ready access to that system. All necessary software should be installed where they can access it, and everyone should have usernames and passwords. Coordinating with whoever may be responsible for the technology or computer system will be an important part of building a successful training program.

When technology resources are out of your control, or perhaps if you've been asked to launch a training program weeks (or months) before a system has been rolled out, then taking advantage of informal learning assets—such as handouts, user manuals, quick reference guides, and checklists—will be essential.

Supervisors Are Ambivalent or Unengaged

There will be times when a supervisor neither knows about nor cares about the training programs your learners complete. Supervisors are busy, and oftentimes, supervising team members is only part of their job. They also have meetings to attend, budgets to assemble and reconcile, operational duties to perform, high performers to keep engaged, and low performers to remediate.

In short, supervisors may not have a lot of time, energy, or knowledge about how to support or hold their employees accountable for using what they've learned through your training program. Ambivalent or unengaged supervisors

Chapter 4

are a problem. According to research from Mary Broad and John Newstrom (1992) in their book *Transfer of Training: Action-Packed Strategies to Ensure High Payoff From Training Investment*, supervisors are the most important factor in determining whether people will apply lessons learned from training.

Finding ways to engage supervisors and help them help their employees can go a long way toward the success of your training program. Any of these suggestions may prove useful in getting your learners' supervisors to support the learning after they've completed the learning experience:

- **Provide a checklist.** Checklists are used every day for everything from to-do lists to following procedures. They make it easy to identify a task, mark that the task has been completed, and then move on to the next task. Coming up with actions that your learners should be doing—based upon your initial learning objectives—and putting them into a checklist can ensure that a supervisor doesn't need to know much (or anything at all) about your training program to support it. Supervisors can simply read through the checklist with their direct reports during a routine one-on-one meeting and easily engage in conversations around being accountable for taking action.

- **Create a rubric.** A simple way to think of a rubric is as grading sheet that lists a specific skill or competency, and then, in separate columns, describes objectively observable behaviors that exceed, meet, and fall short of expectations. A rubric will take more time, thought, and energy to put together than a checklist, but it will offer a supervisor much more direction over their ability to observe new behaviors and give feedback on a topic or skill set that they may not be familiar with.

- **Develop a series of questions.** A week or two after completing a training session or an e-learning module, what kind of questions would you ask your learners to determine if they remember the content or are applying any of it? While you may not have access to your learners, their supervisors will. So, why not share that list of questions with their supervisors to help guide their conversations in a one-on-one meeting?

Supervisors Are Actively Against the Learning Program

When I was responsible for new employee orientation at a previous job, I noticed an interesting trend. We were hiring more people, but I was seeing fewer new employees attend the orientation. One team was growing faster than any other, yet I hadn't seen any new employees come through the orientation in months. So, I reached out to the department head.

"Look," she told me (in her famously curt way of addressing her colleagues), "I'm hiring people because I need more people working. I can't sacrifice the first two days of everyone's tenure so that they can sit through a parade of speakers and PowerPoint slides."

Basically, what she meant was, "Brian, my people's time is valuable. And your program doesn't add any value for us." It was a fair point, and I used that feedback to overhaul the new employee orientation. To make a long story short, after that redesign, everyone (including this department head) began to send new hires (and even some people who had been hired months earlier) through the program.

When supervisors are actively not sending people in your target audience through your training program, it may be a sign that you missed something during the analysis phase. But it's never too late to fix it. Tuck away your ego and seek out feedback from influential managers whose opinions you trust.

In the next chapter, I'll go more in depth into how to effectively borrow different stakeholders' time to increase the likelihood of system-wide success for your training program.

A Shoestring Summary

Your organization is a system—each piece is connected to every other piece, even if those connections aren't always easily visible. Although you can build an extremely engaging learning experience, it doesn't mean your program will yield the intended results, and that could be due to the parts of the organizational system that you can't initially see.

Establishing connections and maintaining good relationships with key stakeholders, SMEs, leaders, and managers across the organization can ultimately determine whether you're building an effective learning program.

PART 2
BORROW

If you're not borrowing something, then you're doing instructional design wrong. When you're on a shoestring, you don't have the time or money to do it wrong.

When I was a new instructional designer, I wanted to prove my worth, so I'd often try to put entire projects on my shoulders to show everyone what I could do. However, because learning itself doesn't happen in a vacuum, neither should learning design. While the best learning solutions will involve your focused, creative, research-backed efforts, they will also involve input from key stakeholders who may know the content, audience, or business problem better than you ever will. Also, the best ideas for activities or the most helpful templates to organize your learning program probably already exist in some way, shape, or form. As the saying goes: There is no need to reinvent the wheel.

For these reasons, borrowing will be an essential aspect of instructional design, especially on a shoestring. You'll need to borrow the time and talents of others, and you may want to borrow inspiration from others as well. Part 2 will offer some guidance on how to borrow the right things to give your instructional design the best possible opportunity to succeed.

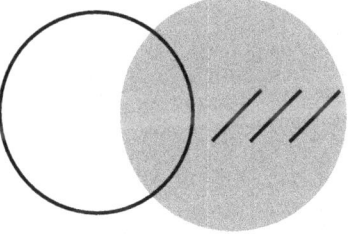

5

Borrowing the Time and Talent of Others

You'll often need to draw on the expertise of others around your organization who are paid to bring their expertise and talents to the organization primarily to do non-training-related things. Even though you may think the training project you're designing is extremely important, that's not how they make money for the organization. So, when you ask them (or when they're told) to spend part of their workday with you, it can be a big ask.

This chapter will focus on four groups of people—SMEs, supervisors, champions, and early testers—that you'll need to borrow time from to ensure your instructional design project has the greatest chance for success. I've briefly talked about each group in earlier chapters, so this chapter will go into more depth about how to engage them.

Working With SMEs

When collecting appropriate content for your learning initiative, you may be able to try several approaches (assuming that you are not an expert in the training program's topic). Sometimes you can find all the information you need through documentation, such as existing PowerPoint files, or through research from within your organization or from external books, journals, magazines, and papers.

Several years ago, shortly after I launched Endurance Learning with a college friend, a new client asked us for some help turning a PowerPoint deck with 319 slides into a multi-day training program. When we looked at the slides, we had no idea which ones contained the most essential information, and we couldn't determine that until we had identified what the learners should be able to do differently or better through the program. Herein is a major shortcoming

87

Chapter 5

of relying solely on documentation to create training—we needed a SME (or two or three) to help us decipher what was in the deck, and what content was most important for the learners.

TOOL

SME Qualification Sheet

If you have any say in the SME whom you'll be working with, then the SME qualification sheet in appendix A, developed by my colleague Heather Barry, may help ensure that you're working with the right person.

SMEs are individuals who have a deep understanding of a specific subject. Sometimes, this experience results from years of specialized schooling in a specific area. Other times, the experience simply accrues over time, through repetition and trial and error. They may have many credentials and sometimes even lofty titles; however, "subject matter expert" is rarely their actual title. You may work with Connie, the director of research, or Dave, the senior sales representative, but you're less likely to work with Connie or Dave, the subject matter expert. SMEs usually have other jobs.

Whether you've had the opportunity to choose a SME or one has been assigned to your project, respect their time. Here are some ways to help you organize your conversations with a SME to be sure you're borrowing their time effectively and getting the information you need to create a meaningful learning experience:

- **Prior to meeting.** These two steps will help ensure that you and the SME are prepared for your meeting and that it will be the most efficient use of everyone's time.
    - Review source materials. If you understand them and the project well enough to ask clarifying questions, then send a list of questions in advance.
    - Provide an agenda. Many SMEs are passionate about their topic and will share anything and everything. As an instructional designer, it will be important for you to give this meeting structure and guide the SMEs on what kind of information will be most helpful.

88

Borrowing the Time and Talent of Others

- **During the meeting.** Different projects will require different levels of effort and information from SMEs. Keep in mind that they have worked for years (or decades or their entire careers) to develop their expertise. While they may find all their knowledge and experience to be essential, the training program you're creating probably isn't designed to convey all their expertise within a two-hour session or 20-minute modules. Your role is to help find and prioritize the most important information and guide the SME toward providing the right information for your project.
  - What should everyone know about this topic?
  - What does it look like when people are performing this skill correctly? What would we see them doing?
  - For this specific skill, what should new learners need to be able to do? (This is your learning objectives question. If the SME says, "They just need to understand X," then you should ask them to complete that sentence. "They just need to understand X so that they can do what?" When working with SMEs, it's extremely important for you to understand the specific behaviors that will result from learners knowing or understanding new information.)
  - What are the three most important things the learners need to know or be able to do? We have so much great source material, but we have limited time with our learners.
  - What is the most challenging part of this skill to learn? Where do people tend to make the most mistakes, especially when they're new to it?
  - When someone does this skill incorrectly, what can happen?
  - How did you learn how to do this skill so well?
  - What is the best sequence and flow for this topic?
  - What kind of checklist, flowchart, or other job aid might help new learners perform this task?
  - Can you help me come up with some realistic scenarios or case studies to help people think critically about this topic or practice demonstrating their new knowledge or skills?
- **Once materials have been drafted.** Getting feedback before your materials go into development or production can save you time and

money on costly edits to the final layout of your training materials or e-learning modules.

- Is there any information missing that learners need? Will it hinder their progress when learning this new skill?
- Is the information shared accurate and in the right sequence and flow?
- Is any information superfluous?
- Are the case studies or practice activities realistic?
- Are the distractors (incorrect choices for multiple choice activities) realistic?

Some SMEs may appreciate structure, but others may prefer a free-flow exchange of ideas. You'll have to decide what works best for your timeline, and more importantly what will work best for the limited time you'll have access to the SMEs.

Working With Supervisors

While your instructional design will focus on your immediate learners, don't forget about the power of their supervisors. Even the most well-intentioned, motivated individual employee will become caught between their desire and enthusiasm to do something new or better and other forces (such as higher priorities, deadlines, deliverables, projects, emails, and meetings) that tend to keep the status quo in place. Who will hold learners accountable for doing something new, different, or better?

Analyzing data from several studies, Broad and Newstrom (1992) assert that when learners aren't supported in their post-training efforts to apply what they've learned to their jobs, the transfer of skills from training to the real world is disappointingly low. No matter how much a learner may want to adopt new knowledge or skills after a training session, their behavior rarely changes—unless they receive additional levels of support. According to the research, barriers to transferring learning from a training environment to the real world include:

- Lack of reinforcement on the job
- Interference from the immediate work environment
- Nonsupportive organizational culture
- Learners' discomfort with change and the effort required for that change

Borrowing the Time and Talent of Others

- Being separated from the inspiration or support a trainer provided during the session
- Pressure from peers to resist the change

In another study, Broad and Newstrom asked training professionals to rank who might be in the best position to help overcome these transfer-to-the-job barriers and when. Although they say that further research should be done, the results are compelling. Broad and Newstrom found that the most important person to help overcome some of these barriers (and provide a better chance for your training program to lead to on-the-job behavior change) is the supervisor—*before* a learner goes through the learning experience, and then again after they've completed it.

Table 5-1 offers some specific strategies that Broad and Newstrom recommend supervisors apply both before and after a training program.

Table 5-1. Involving Supervisors Before and After a Learning Experience

Before a Learning Experience	Following a Learning Experience
• Collect baseline performance data. • Offer coaching and set goals. • Offer rewards and incentives. • Select the appropriate learners for the appropriate learning experiences. • Send co-workers through a learning experience together. • Provide time to complete pre-course assignments. • Encourage participation in all learning experiences.	• Identify and provide opportunities for applying the skills in the real world. • Schedule time for the learners to share what they learned with colleagues. • Provide role models. • Give reinforcement. • Set mutual expectations for improvement. • Provide and support use of job aids. • Support learner reunions. • Publicize successes. • Provide incentives and promotional preference.

I've found that when a supervisor approaches me to say, "We need some help, possibly some training," it's much easier to do many of the pre- and post-learning action items with them. Things such as getting buy-in for learners to schedule time on their calendars to complete prework, setting goals and clear expectations for their team in advance of a learning experience, gathering baseline performance data, offering support and reinforcement after a session, and

Chapter 5

following up with learners are low-hanging fruit for a supervisor who's already bought in to the need for a learning program.

Even when supervisors aren't part of the driving force behind a learning program, sending a goal-setting and reflection document to learners by email in advance of a program can be an effective way of priming the learning pump for attendees while also engaging their supervisors in the process.

Broad and Newstrom's research is both interesting and important for on-the-job success and impact of training programs. Have you ever supervised someone? Have you ever supervised a team? If so, you'd know that people management is challenging work. Some employees are high achievers and want to be challenged. Some lag behind what's expected and take time and energy to be coached to meet expectations. Others are struggling with conflicts with other team members or things happening outside work. Still others consistently drop hints—overtly or subtly—about how they'd like a promotion or raise.

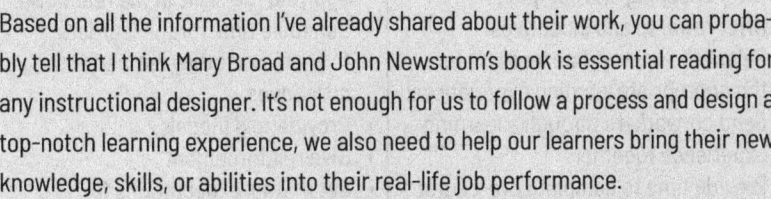

DEEPER DIVE
Transferring Training to On-the-Job Performance

Based on all the information I've already shared about their work, you can probably tell that I think Mary Broad and John Newstrom's book is essential reading for any instructional designer. It's not enough for us to follow a process and design a top-notch learning experience, we also need to help our learners bring their new knowledge, skills, or abilities into their real-life job performance.

- Mary L. Broad and John W. Newstrom, *Transfer of Training: Action-Packed Strategies to Ensure High Payoff From Training Investments* (New York: Basic Books, 1992).

Managers also face pressure from their own supervisors in meeting team performance metrics or hitting budget goals (or making budget cuts). Furthermore, they typically have their own jobs to do as well. Asking supervisors to support a learning initiative so that learners will transfer what they've learned to the real world is often seen as just one more thing for a supervisor to prioritize, and in my experience, it's typically a low priority.

Instructional designers may be limited by what a supervisor will do to support the learners, but you are not completely powerless. The key is to include supervisor support strategies in the initial analysis and design phases and make sure that anything involving a supervisor is a low-lift effort that can be easily adopted or implemented.

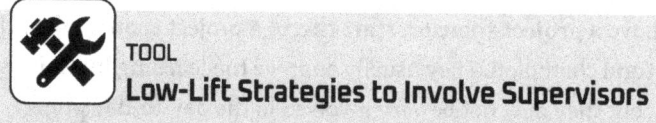

TOOL
Low-Lift Strategies to Involve Supervisors

In appendix A, you'll find a checklist of low-lift strategies for involving stakehold-ers. While you don't need to do every strategy each time you develop a learning initiative, using one or a combination of strategies can help your learners' super-visors help you increase the likelihood that learning will be transferred to the job.

Finding Champions

On social media platforms, they're known as "influencers"—people who promote products or brands and make them seem cool, thus attracting others to buy them. In professional sports, they're known as "hype men" (or hype women)—people who can attract new fans and get the crowd cheering for an athlete or team. In organizations, I'll call them "champions."

In chapter 4, I wrote about the importance of Jen, the operations team lead, and how her enthusiastic praise of my instructional design process led more people to immediately buy in to good training design than I could have ever done in a lifetime of working for that company. Jen is the kind of champion I'm talking about.

Just because you believe in the learning experience you're building, no one will be as passionate as you are. Just because you've come up with the most creative, interactive, and downright amazing idea to present a concept or teach a new skill, learners won't flock to your program (and supervisors won't clamor to use their time to support it). You need someone to serve as your champion.

Who are your champions?

- Respected executives, such as your company's CEO
- Influential department heads

Chapter 5

- Managers or individual contributors who seem to know everyone
- A SME that everyone in your company goes to and trusts

How do you establish good relationships with champions around your organization? A good relationship means you won't have to awkwardly ask them out of the blue if they'll put in a good word about your learning initiative. Here are a few tips:

- **If you have a project sponsor, start there.** A project sponsor should be a natural champion. They usually approve the learning initiative's budget, but they may not be very involved in the day-to-day project management or development. If they're a high-profile person within the organization, they can easily get the word out about how great this learning opportunity will be. Make sure the project sponsor is equipped to offer some messaging about your learning initiative by feeding them key talking points.

- **Never eat lunch at your desk.** This one is tough if you're as introverted as I am. It's even more difficult if you work remotely or as part of a dispersed work team (but it's not impossible). I often see lunchtime as an opportunity to recharge my batteries by putting some food in my body and not talking with anyone for a few minutes. Over the years, however, I've found that strong relationships can be made by spending time with co-workers outside the meeting room. We can talk about nonwork things and appreciate each other beyond our work lives. People are a lot more willing to support my work initiatives when they know me on a deeper level. Plus, lunch conversations often include plenty of complaints, which can reveal immediate learning needs or provide insights into what organizational barriers might prevent future learning initiatives from succeeding. This takes more effort when you're working virtually, but throwing time on the calendar to come together as a team with virtual meeting software, without any other agenda than to talk about how things are going (at work and beyond) can pay huge dividends.

- **Grab coffee.** Getting out of the office environment can be an important way to develop a relationship with key people in your organization. Your project sponsor, influential mid-level leaders, or key senior leaders will remember the time you took to have coffee and learn more about their concerns and how learning initiatives might be able to support them. This will be helpful later when you ask them to hype your next learning initiative (or when you need funding). Make sure you have an agenda because the higher up a person is on the org chart, the less time they may have for chit chat.

- **Support others' work.** Being a champion can go both ways. If you can promote and support the work of others around your organization, do it. This could take many forms, from providing a thoughtful comment on a colleague's LinkedIn post to showing up when a project sponsor coordinates a brown-bag lunch session on a topic completely unrelated to your training program. People generally remember who supported them and don't have a problem returning the favor down the road.

Finding Pilot Groups and Beta Testers

"That was good." "I liked it." "Wow, that might be the coolest training experience I've ever had the pleasure of participating in." When it comes to qualitative feedback, all three of those comments might fall into the category of *vanity metrics*—comments that make you feel good about your learning initiative and feed your ego. But they don't tell you anything about what specifically about the program is good (or what specifically needs to be tightened up) before your initiative is implemented for the masses.

Identifying the right people, and then borrowing their time to get the most useful and actionable feedback during a pilot run of your ILT program or beta test of your e-learning module, can be the difference between a smooth roll-out and one that yields disappointing initial results.

Some people you might want to consider engaging to test your learning program include:

- Colleagues who you are confident will offer honest feedback about the good, the bad, and the ugly
- A sampling of your target audience
- SMEs
- Some (or all) of the people who may need to deliver an ILT program

Chapter 5

Here are some questions you may want to ask to ensure the feedback you get is targeted and actionable:

- What were your key takeaways, and what did you think was the intent of this learning experience?
- When you compare the learning objectives with the activities and content in the learning experience, do you think the learning objectives were accomplished?
- What did you like about this learning experience?
- Where did you struggle during this learning experience?
- Were the instructions for activities clear?

You may also want feedback on grammar, spelling, and terminology, but ideally this shouldn't be where the pilot group or beta testers focus their time and attention. If you have an editor or someone else who can review your materials specifically for grammar, spelling, and terminology, then your testing group can put their undivided attention on the effectiveness of your design.

 TOOL
Ensuring You Get the Feedback You Need

In appendix A, you'll find an email my colleague Lauren Wescott sent to a client when it was time for them to review the first draft of an e-learning module. I've removed some details and made it more generic, but you may wish to use this as a template the next time you're looking for feedback on a learning initiative.

A Shoestring Summary

While part of the instructional design process is about crafting an engaging learning experience using sound instructional design practices, forging strong interpersonal relationships is another key aspect of instructional design.

Using your SMEs' time in a respectful and efficient way not only ensures you're getting the content that you need, but also means that you're using it in the best way possible. Find opportunities to engage your learners' supervisors; it can mean the difference between a learning program that people find interesting and a learning program that yields results. Champions can be found all around your organization; they can help promote your learning program to increase exposure and completions and perhaps even help fund future projects. Finding the right people to test out your learning programs and asking them the right questions to ensure you get actionable feedback is another part of the instructional design process that should not be overlooked or shortchanged.

6
Borrowing Inspiration From Everywhere

In spring 2019, I was having lunch with my oldest child when I noticed their placemat, which looked like a small version of the periodic table. Instead of elements like Hydrogen and Helium, it had elements like Local Beef and Oreo Shake, which were consistent with the restaurant's theme—Lunchbox Laboratory.

As I stared at this version of the periodic table, an idea came to me: Wouldn't it be fun to create a periodic table of learning elements? So, I did.

The periodic table in Figure 6-1, on the next page, is the heart of my first book, *What's Your Formula? Combine Learning Elements for Impactful Training*. I was proud of myself for coming up with such a creative, original idea. Who else could have thought of a periodic table for learning?

However, there's a problem with this line of thinking—this idea wasn't original. As I've already mentioned (and if you've completed middle school science, you probably already know), there was a periodic table of elements long before I had this idea. And others were already using periodic tables in their own industries, as illustrated by the placemat on my child's corn dog tray. Even in my own industry, Andrzej Marczewski published his Periodic Table of Gamification Elements in 2017, and ELB Learning released a periodic table of instructional design in 2020.

So what's the solution? Embrace it! Welcome to the chapter in which I'll encourage you to stop trying to be original, and instead borrow inspiration from other sources or experiences that already exist.

Chapter 6

Figure 6-1. Endurance Learning's Elements of Amazing Learning Experiences

Endurance Learning's
Elements of Amazing Learning Experiences

☐ Solid Elements ☐ Gas-like Elements ☐ Radioactive Elements
☐ Liquid Elements ☐ Interactive Elements

Lp Lesson Plan								Su Supervisor Support
Wd Word	Re Audience Response				Lc Lecture	Pp PowerPoint	Me Measuring for Effectiveness	Lb Learning Boosts
Qz Quiz Software	Gg Google	Vi Video	Al Adult Learning	De Dialogue Education	Ex Subject Matter Experts	Hn Handouts	Sl Spaced Learning	Fu Follow Up
Vm Virtual Meeting	Ms Mc Sketch Markers	Fc Flipchart	Gm Gamification	Cm Change Management	Sm Smile Sheets	Ib Icebreakers	As Assessment	Mn Mentorship
Ra Rapid Authoring	Sc Screen Capture	Sr Screen Recording	Le Levels of Evaluation	Vd Visual Design	El Elearning	Ar Augmented Reality	Co Coaching	Mc Microlearning
Sb Soapbox	Cf Collaborative File Sharing	Tt Text Tools	Lo Learning Objectives Taxonomy	Id Instructional Design	Rp Role Play	Ga Games	Dt Data	Gs Goal Setting
		Tw Twitter	Li LinkedIn	Bl Blog	Wb Website	Yt YouTube	Sh Slideshare	Em Email

endurance

Source: Endurance Learning. Used with permission.

It's OK to Borrow!

When I first began writing lesson plans as a GED instructor, I didn't know what I was doing. I wanted to give my students a learning experience that the traditional education system had not been able to offer them. I wanted to be original in thought and activity. But I often found myself staring at a blank computer screen. I just couldn't get new ideas to flow.

My father, who had been teaching science for most of his career, was frequently requested by parents because he had a reputation for keeping kids engaged when learning tricky science concepts. Sometimes, he would share lesson plans with me, but I wasn't sure if I should be stealing his ideas. When I mentioned to him that I liked his ideas but wanted to be original for my students, he let me in on one of his greatest secrets as an instructional designer: "Brian, there are no new ideas, just borrowed ones. So, use any lesson plan of mine that you think will help your students get their GEDs!"

Borrowing Inspiration From Everywhere

Take all the ideas you can from this chapter. However, whether you're borrowing these ideas or are inspired to search online for other ideas that are more aligned with your content areas, be sure to give appropriate attribution. I've found many people can be generous with their ideas, but it's in poor taste (and unethical and sometimes illegal) to claim someone else's work as your own.

Inspiration truly is all around us. You just need to stop and look around, with intent, and be open to ideas that may land in your lap. Let's discuss some possible sources of intentional inspiration.

Museums

Museums are a surprisingly good sources of inspiration for training and instructional design. Whether you have access to a children's museum, a specialty museum (like a spy museum or one dedicated to a specific topic), a community museum, or an art gallery, plan a visit with the intent of finding inspiration for your next project. Or, if you've visited one recently, think about your experience walking through the exhibits.

The museum exhibits that you view (and often interact with) don't just show up. They have been carefully and thoughtfully designed by an exhibit designer. According to Museum Environments, a company that specializes in exhibit design, the "ideal museum experience is transformative and all-encompassing. It is experiential in the fullest sense because of its multi-dimensional quality. The experience happens between people (audience), places (museums), and things (exhibits). A successful museum experience must cover all these spaces simultaneously." Museum Environments put this concept of an ideal museum visit into the Venn diagram in Figure 6-2 on the next page.

If you replaced "exhibits" with "learner engagement strategies" and "museum mission" with "learning objectives," this Venn diagram could be a good road map for creating an effective learning experience.

After visiting a museum, ask yourself these questions to help transfer some of your experience to your instructional design:

- Who is the museum's (or a specific exhibit's) intended audience?
- How does the museum cater exhibits to its audience?
- How does the sequence and flow of exhibits augment the experience?
- How does a particular exhibit use technology to engage the audience?

Chapter 6

- What instructions are visitors given to help them make the most of their experience?
- What job aids (such as maps or audio tours) can visitors use to enhance their experience?
- What clever devices are used to help visitors learn about a topic or an exhibit?
- Which exhibits did you spend the most time visiting? Why?
- Did you walk away knowing something that you didn't know before you entered the museum? How did your experience help you to learn or understand that new nugget of information?

Figure 6-2. Museum Environments' Venn Diagram

Source: Museum Environments. Used with permission.

Borrowing Inspiration From Everywhere

TIME SAVER
Exploring Museums Without Leaving Home

If you want to draw inspiration from museums but don't have time to visit one, many museums—including the Smithsonian and the Louvre—have websites with virtual tours and interactive exhibits that you can explore.

In addition, you can visit Google's Arts & Culture site (artsandculture.google.com) to explore museums, play museum-related games, and interact in other ways.

Advertising and Marketing

Similar to museum exhibit design, the process for designing marketing and advertising content holds a number of lessons for instructional designers. When you think of your role as an instructional designer, part of your job is to help people find the urgency or motivation to engage with your learning experience. Professionals in the advertising and marketing industry are particularly adept at this.

Danielle Wallace (2021) was once responsible for major advertising campaigns at Procter and Gamble and PepsiCo and now runs Beyond the Sky, a customer learning solutions company. She says marketing and advertising companies do three things well:

- Use compelling visuals to better depict the message.
- Accompany visuals with extremely concise text.
- Find ways to tap into our emotions.

Whether you're borrowing inspiration for a story narrative that can run through a learning program or ways to offer a more compelling visual experience, take a look around. Look at billboards and magazine ads. Pay attention to the commercials on TV. Yes, they're trying to sell you car insurance or cell phone service, but they're not just saying, "Our cell phone service uses the latest technology, so sign up with us!" That's not a very compelling narrative.

I recently heard a radio ad that begins with a man's voice asking, "Already?!" Then, you hear him typing a text message. His phone's digital voice feature reads the reply he receives as he drives. Later, you hear him burst into a hospital delivery room and say, "Honey, I'm here!" This cell phone company isn't just trying to sell me a two-year contract; they're selling me the security and peace of mind that comes with knowing I can communicate with a whole world of people in different ways, especially during important times, with *their* service.

The next time you decide to look at marketing and advertising content for inspiration for your instructional design, ask yourself:

- What elements can I transfer from the way imagery appears on a billboard or magazine ad to the way I design a visual story in my PowerPoint slides or e-learning module?
- What is it about the way information is presented that makes me enjoy, appreciate, and *want* to see some ads again, while others are either forgettable or make me want to change the station?
- What information have advertisers chosen to leave out or omit because they had to ruthlessly limit their message to 30 seconds? Would the ad have been more powerful if it lasted five minutes instead of 30 seconds?

Co-Workers and Colleagues

Remember that you don't need to work in isolation, even if it feels like you're the only instructional designer for miles around. Sometimes, speaking with someone who is not an instructional designer can help clear your mind and move you beyond your instructional designer's block.

I have one co-worker who will call me and ask if he can bounce some ideas around with me. He'll talk at me for 30 minutes or so, and I'll nod and smile, but I'll never get a word in edgewise (which is for the best because they're usually about some technical topic I'm clueless about). At the end of our call, he'll say, "Wow, that was helpful. Thank you!" Sometimes, it can be helpful to simply talk through an idea aloud.

During our weekly Endurance Learning team meetings, we allocate time specifically to brainstorm ideas for specific projects. (We actually call our team meetings "play dates" because they are intended to be a time for us to come together and share ideas as opposed to traditional team meetings that revolve around announcements and reports.) When nobody on the team needs help brainstorming activities or design ideas for a project, we'll ask everyone to come with show-and-tell items. Even though we're a small team, we're very busy, and we don't always have time to see what other people are working on.

Borrowing Inspiration From Everywhere

Setting aside an hour or so a month for each team member to share some of their most creative solutions to training challenges helps spark ideas for projects that other people are working on. At these show-and-tell play dates, one team member will often ask another if they can borrow an activity or a template for their own project. So, someone on your team, in your organization, or perhaps in your community of practice may have already come up with an idea or activity that can solve a challenge you're working on.

Communities of Practice and Professional Associations

A *community of practice (COP)* is a group of people who hold the same job responsibilities and meet on a regular basis to share and discuss promising practices, challenges, obstacles, and ways to improve. A *professional association* consists of people working in the same field and usually requires paid membership. You might be a member of one already.

I've belonged to several COPs, and I found the benefits to be invaluable. One COP was internal to my organization—because there wasn't a central training department or chief learning officer, trainers from across the organization came together to form this community. During some meetings, individual members were responsible for bringing training challenges to the group, and the entire group would brainstorm creative ways to overcome the challenges. During other meetings, the group would help someone outline a training project they had coming up, or several group members would volunteer to do a short presentation on a topic that could help all of us—such as training basics like lesson plan design or technical topics specific to the group member's department.

Another COP I continue to be involved with is a group of trainers and facilitators from around the world who meet virtually, once a month. A general benefit of being involved with this group is that I leave every meeting more energized from talking with "my people" and learning about some of the projects they're working on. Specifically, when I had writer's block while working on a chapter I had committed to write for a different book, I brought my challenge to the group, and they filled me with ideas.

Larger organizations may have a COP for trainers and instructional designers (or perhaps after reading this, you may be inspired to create one). If you work

Chapter 6

in a smaller organization, you may want to find an external COP or reach out to other instructional designers in your network to assemble your own group.

Professional associations for instructional designers include groups like the Association for Talent Development (ATD) and its local chapters. If you're mainly involved with instructional design for e-learning projects, then the Learning Guild may be a group worth exploring. While almost all professional associations have an annual membership fee, you may find ideas and inspiration from their conferences, webinars, or the connections you make.

Games

In her book *Reality Is Broken: Why Games Make Us Better and How They Can Change the World*, Jane McGonigal (2011) writes about the benefits that gameplay can bring into your next learning experience. She also talks about the four core properties of games:

- They have a goal.
- They have rules.
- They have a feedback system (like earning points for doing something right or dying when a creeper finds you because you haven't built enough fortifications).
- Participation is voluntary.

Keep in mind that *games* and *gamification* are two different things. A *game* is a specific learning *activity* in which game elements are used to accomplish specific learning objectives. *Gamification*, on the other hand, is an instructional design *strategy* that combines intention with a coherent collection of game elements to produce an engaging learning experience connected to objectives and outcomes.

Whether you're applying gamification to an entire instructional design project or borrowing inspiration for a specific activity draw inspiration from games that already exist. However, you should do more than just peruse Amazon or the aisles at Target to see what games are available; actually playing the games is important so you can experience which game mechanics work for you. You might begin with what you have at home. What is it about games like *Candyland*, *Uno*, *Monopoly*, and *Risk* that keeps people coming back?

Borrowing Inspiration From Everywhere

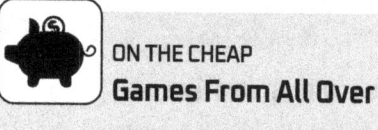

ON THE CHEAP
Games From All Over

If you want to discover new game mechanics (and perhaps new worlds), see if your local coffee shop, game store, or bar has a game library. Grab some friends and try a game you haven't played before. Local thrift stores are another place to find inexpensive (and unfamiliar) games. You can also check the app store on your phone for popular games. One of my colleagues once came up with an effective learning solution for an e-learning project based on the game *Angry Birds*.

While using games and gamification may sound like a fun idea, remember that game design (like museum exhibit design) is an entire discipline. The reason store-bought games are so fun and seem to flow naturally is because someone (or an entire team) devoted a ton of time to mapping out how the game should flow, prototyping different versions, and refining it.

When you borrow inspiration from a game, keep some of these questions in mind:

- What learning objectives can learners accomplish using this game or game elements?
- What makes the instructions for setting up and playing the game so helpful?
- How does the game create tension and conflict?
- Do players work together or compete against one another? (This is an important question to answer and game mechanic to observe. If you're working on a training program in which people need to work together to solve a problem, then you'll want to find inspiration from a cooperative game.)
- How does the gameplay provide feedback to the players?
- If you win, would you want to play this game again? If you played exactly the same way again, would you win again, or would you need to adjust your strategy?
- If you lose, would you want to play this game again so you could find a way to win?

Chapter 6

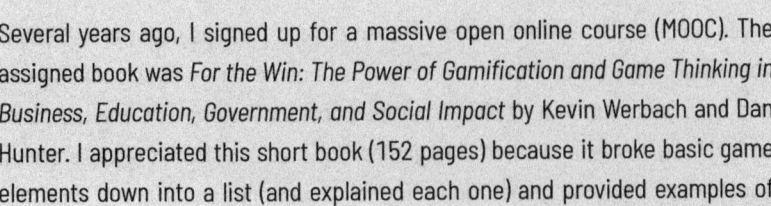

DEEPER DIVE
Gamification of Your Learning Initiative

Several years ago, I signed up for a massive open online course (MOOC). The assigned book was *For the Win: The Power of Gamification and Game Thinking in Business, Education, Government, and Social Impact* by Kevin Werbach and Dan Hunter. I appreciated this short book (152 pages) because it broke basic game elements down into a list (and explained each one) and provided examples of what gamification looked like in different real-world contexts.

I still revisit the list of game elements in this book so that I don't always default to the same ones everyone else uses (like points, badges, and leaderboards).

If you're looking for additional gamification resources, I'd also recommend:
- Jane McGonigal, *Reality Is Broken: Why Games Make Us Better and How They Can Change the World* (New York: Penguin, 2011).
- Karl M. Kapp, *The Gamification of Learning and Instruction: Game-Based Methods and Strategies for Training and Education* (San Francisco: Pfeiffer, 2012).

The Internet

There is a whole world of training projects, instructional design samples, templates, AI-created lessons, images, and PowerPoint slide decks at your fingertips. One Google search can deliver millions of results in less than a second. Can you search for "training activities"? Yes, you can. When you're working on a shoestring—whether tight on time or money—this is particularly tempting. Unfortunately, Google does not (yet) have a filter for *effective* training activity examples, so you'll need to be careful when borrowing inspiration from the internet.

Finding activities is one thing, but deciding how they unfold in your learning experience is another. When searching online, you should hold on to your instructional design fundamentals. In chapter 2, I wrote about the Anchor-Content-Application-Future Use model that I always use to design a progression of activities. When you search for "training activities," know which step

Borrowing Inspiration From Everywhere

you want to fulfill with an activity and how it will relate to other parts of your program and your learning objectives.

Here are some specific places you may want to search for inspiration, examples, and templates:

- **Training company websites.** Many have portfolios of projects you can draw inspiration from.
- **Pinterest.** There are many teaching and instructional design boards that offer ideas.
- **Articulate's E-Learning Heroes website.** The site includes Q&A forums, tutorials, templates, and even downloadable Storyline files for both basic and complex e-learning interactions.
- **Companies that specialize in technical services.** These can be resources for content and ways to present the content.
- **YouTube.** You can find examples of tutorials, webcasts, instructional videos, and creative ways others are presenting content and information.

DEEPER DIVE
Ensuring the Veracity of Content From the Internet

You may want to also keep Molly Beestrum's CRAP Test in mind while searching the internet for inspiration. This aptly named test suggests that you should think about four elements of any website that you're tempted to draw inspiration from:

- **Currency.** How up to date is the information?
- **Reliability.** Are you drawing upon opinion, research, or conspiracy theories?
- **Authority.** Who is the source?
- **Purpose and point of view.** What is the motivation behind the information?

To protect your credibility (and that of your learning program), taking a few minutes to review information you find on the internet can make a big difference. These resources will help you run your own CRAP (or CRAAP) test:

- "Evaluating Sources Toolkit: CRAP Test." cccs.libguides.com/CRAPTest.
- "Evaluating Information—Applying the CRAAP Test," Meriam Library California State University, Chico, September 17, 2010, library.csuchico .edu/sites/default/files/craap-test.pdf.

109

Chapter 6

Use the internet to find templates, checklists, or forms that you can use to organize your content. Keep in mind that if you do borrow imagery or other intellectual property, you must provide the proper attribution.

A Shoestring Summary

As you can see, sources of inspiration that you can borrow resources from come in many shapes and sizes. My team and I even spent time watching the movie *Jumanji* (the original Robin Williams's version) before we redesigned our company's new employee orientation program—and it inspired visions of an immersive game that began to dance in our heads.

Instructional designers will wear many hats, but there is nothing in our job description that says we need to come up with an original idea for every single project. As you look to shorten the time it takes to put together learning programs, find inspiration from others through a community of practice, professional association, or team meeting to help get you started. Explore a museum, a game, or even the internet with the intent to borrow the design mechanics from others' work into your own learning initiatives, especially sites like Articulate's E-Learning Heroes, which offers templates and source codes you can download for free!

PART 3
BUY

When you're operating on a shoestring, you might not have the budget to purchase tools, resources, or services to design your learning experiences. But I encourage you to not skip this part. Even if you have a limited budget, there may still be some pieces that make sense for you to purchase. If you're running short on time, some of what you find in this section may prove extremely helpful.

As I've written throughout this book, "on a shoestring" may mean that you're limited on resources, such as time or money, or that you need to tackle an aspect of instructional design you're less knowledgeable about. If you have *absolutely no* money to spend on any part of your training program—whether that's an inexpensive survey tool or even a rapid authoring tool to develop an e-learning course—then this part of the book may not help you solve your current instructional design challenges. The ideas, however, might help plant the seeds for a future project.

If you have a modest budget, read on and you may find some elements you can use. Whether you're looking for something that will make your instructional design a little easier, an extra set of hands to help, or a learning program that already exists, this part is designed to help you find the best way to pay for what you need.

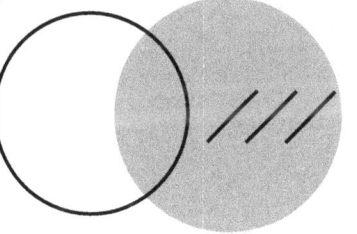

7
Paying for Convenience

Time is money. When you're operating on a shoestring budget, it's tempting to say, "We can't afford to spend money on anything for this learning initiative, and because my time is free, I'll have to create everything myself." However, your time isn't free. For example, if you make $70,000 a year, your organization is investing a little over $33 an hour for each hour you spend working on an instructional design project. The average loaded rate (including taxes, benefits, and overhead) is about 24 percent higher than what's reflected in your salary agreement, so a salary of $70,000 a year actually costs your employer $86,800, or about $48 an hour.

Keep this in mind the next time you spend eight hours Googling and watching YouTube to figure out how to create an e-learning interaction or set up PowerPoint to branch just the right way for your game of *Jeopardy*. You just spent $384 of your employer's money. Would a better investment have been purchasing a downloadable *Jeopardy* template or game?

Use the flowchart on the next page to decide whether this part of the book will be beneficial for you (Figure 7-1).

This chapter will offer some ideas for when you may want to pay for automated solutions or services instead of doing everything on your own. Your project may benefit from some combination of the ideas in this chapter, or it may not. It will be up to you to decide, but it's tough to make any decisions when you don't know what's available. Table 7-1 offers some examples to think about.

Chapter 7

Figure 7-1. Decision Tree for Buying Decisions

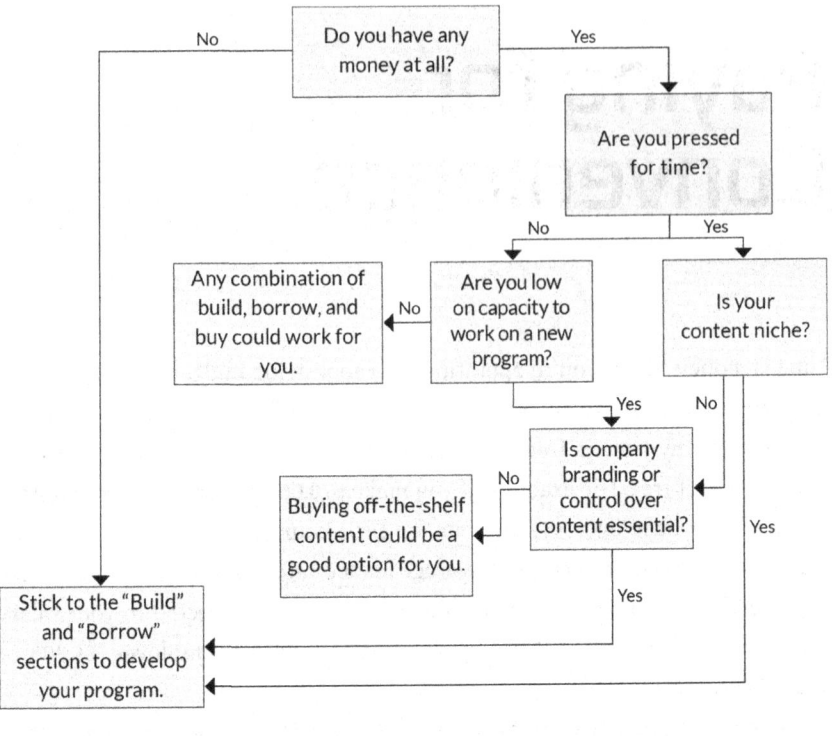

Table 7-1. The Trade-Offs of Doing It Yourself Versus Using Available Tools

Do-It-Yourself Strategy	Available Tools and Services
Use voting dots and flipcharts.	Use a survey platform that integrates into your slides and projects on the screen.
Develop a *Jeopardy* game using PowerPoint (or a flipchart).	Use a classroom gaming platform.
Read a book on how to create more effective visual aids.	Use slide or graphic design software.
Teach yourself basic coding skills or use e-learning tools installed in your organization's LMS.	Use rapid authoring tools.
Create animations with PowerPoint.	Use animation software.

114

Paying for Convenience

Table 7-1. The Trade-Offs of Doing It Yourself Versus Using Available Tools (Cont.)

Do-It-Yourself Strategy	Available Tools and Services
Run text through Google translate (and hope it accurately translates).	Use a translation service.
Record and edit voice-overs (if you have audio editing software).	Use a voice-over artist or software with automated voice-over capability.

As you read this chapter, keep in mind that even some DIY solutions include costs that go beyond your free time (or perhaps your prepaid time). It may even cost more to purchase flipcharts or books to learn how to do something than it would to buy available tools and services (that may also make your life easier). Because the tools and services I cover in this chapter range in price from free to expensive, I've also included how much money you can expect to spend when paying for convenience—you'll see $ (cheap), $$ (moderate), and $$$ (expensive).

 ON THE CHEAP
Free Versions and Trials

Some tools and services have a free version (with limited functionality), and most offer a free trial so you can try before you buy. If you work for a nonprofit organization or an educational institution, you may also be eligible for reduced pricing.

Quiz, Gaming, and Survey Platforms ($–$$)

Quiz, gaming, and survey software allow you to easily create assets to integrate into PowerPoint slide decks or simply project onto a screen as part of ILT course. They can be free or moderate in cost depending on the number of learners who will be using the tools. Most of these services can be paid for as a single-use event or as a subscription service.

Why Pay for It?

While using voting dots, a simple show of hands, or the polling feature of your virtual training platform will work for many activities, there are times when you'll ask a question that may yield better data if participants are given

Chapter 7

anonymity. The examples in Figure 7-2 highlight the use of polling software during an executive retreat in which we needed to get input from all participants quickly yet anonymously.

Figure 7-2. Examples of Polling Your Audience

Assuming we maintain a vision statement, it should...

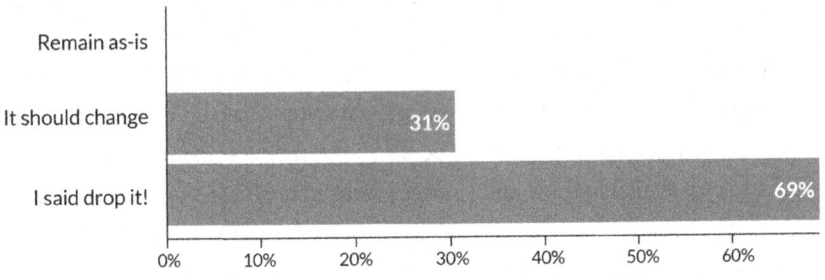

If we were to add to or revise our vision statement, what needs to be added or revised?

The first image presents poll results that the leaders might not have felt comfortable answering by raising their hands. The second image is a word cloud based on input from the group, with the larger words mentioned more often. Capturing this information through a running tally is time consuming for you (or your producer); your time is better spent reflecting on the substance of the answers.

What if your learning design needs a trivia game as an anchor or application activity? While can create it on your own, there are some slick and free or low-cost options available that allow you to enter your questions and answers into the software, which takes care of the rest. If you need data points to track whether people are getting the right answers, many of these software programs also allow you to generate reports on who answered which questions correctly.

Rapid Authoring Tools ($$$)

Rapid authoring tools are software designed for the quick and easy development of a learning program without the need for advanced coding skills.

Why Pay for It?

At this point, I don't think many of you reading this book would go out and learn how to code an e-learning module because your boss asked you to create one. Too many people, however, are stuck using the limited e-learning tools that are included with their company's LMS. If all the tool allows you to do is give people information and perhaps a quiz at the end of a course, I recommend that you return to some of the earlier chapters of this book. Yes, using tools with limited functionality technically qualifies as e-learning content, but if you're not able to design a learning experience that leaves your learners able to remember new content or do something new, differently, or better, was it a good use of anyone's time (even if it was free to develop)?

Rapid authoring tools—such as Articulate Rise, Articulate Storyline, Adobe Captivate, Lectora, and isEazy—provide an easy-to-use interface. With practice, you can generate learning experiences that range from straightforward to choose-your-own-adventure branching scenarios (and everything in between).

Visual Design Software ($–$$)

Visual design software can help you create slides and materials that look professional without advanced training or a degree in graphic design.

Why Pay for It?

One of my favorite resources on the internet is Jesse Desjardins's viral slide deck "You Suck At PowerPoint!" The title is blunt, but for most of us (myself included), it's true. PowerPoint is a powerful tool that is used almost universally, yet unless you have top-notch visual design skills, you may never access its full potential. Should people be more interested in your instructional design than your visual design? In theory, yes. But there's no denying that people are drawn to slick, pretty visual aids, slides, and materials.

Furthermore, have you ever tried wrestling with the placement of images in a Word document when all you were trying to do was make one small edit? Microsoft Word is not a visual design tool. While some talented individuals can make anything in Word or PowerPoint look amazing, most of us visual design amateurs need some additional help.

Tools like Canva, which can range in price from free to a monthly or annual subscription, offer templates, fonts, and images that go beyond the standard tools like PowerPoint that you may have at your fingertips. When creating handouts or guides, you may also want to look into a tool such as Adobe InDesign, which will be both more powerful and more expensive than free or moderately priced software.

Animation Software ($$)

Animation software uses custom artwork and cartoons so you can create explainer videos, tutorials, and other content without the need for advanced coding or animation skills.

Why Pay for It?

One of my LinkedIn contacts once posted a series of animated videos he created using PowerPoint. They illustrated just how powerful a tool PowerPoint can be if you have the time and skill set to develop cool things like that. For the rest of us, tools such as PowToon or Vyond are low cost, easy-to-use options. Short cartoon videos can often illustrate concepts in a more engaging way than a traditional e-learning module, which might simply involve scrolling or clicking through concepts on a screen.

There's another major advantage to using animated characters to explain a concept as opposed to videoing someone in your office talking about the same concept—animated characters usually stay evergreen for longer stretches of time. If the the employee on your video decides to move on to a different company, you may need to rerecord and rerelease a new video.

Translation Services ($–$$$)

Translation services often provide a collection of professionals who can translate your content into any language so your organization can reach every learner.

Why Pay for It?

Your organization may have native speakers of other languages who can help translate your content. Or, perhaps you speak another language and can translate the content yourself. In some cases, this will suffice. However, what if

Paying for Convenience

your go-to in-house translator (like any other SME) is busy with other work and has limited or inconsistent availability? That could ultimately kill your project's timeline. Professional translation services will also offer more consistent translations of your content than you would get if you used two or more in-house resources.

Pricing for translation services varies widely because they typically charge per word—the more content you need translated, the more you'll pay.

Voice-Over Service ($–$$$)

Professional voice actors are available to record and provide digital files of voice-overs for e-learning content, videos, or other training assets.

Why Pay for It?

You can record all the voice-overs for your projects in-house, and when you're operating on a shoestring and have the time, that may be the best way to go. However, recording voice-overs also means ensuring the recorded audio is clean. Learners do not want to hear any "uhs" and "uhms" when listening to voice-overs, and they want audio quality that doesn't sound tinny, echoey, or breathy.

Professional voice-over artists will record and edit content faster than most of us, so if you're short on time, this service could be a good investment. You can also find talented voice-over artists on LinkedIn or through freelance sites, such as Fiverr. The more content you need recorded in a voice-over, the more you'll pay.

Pricing for voice-over services varies widely because they typically charge per word.

TOOL

Options for Paying for Convenience

If you're looking for some tools that can help you put together your next learning program, check out the list of web-based applications in appendix A. They may help make your training more effective and engaging for your learners and easier for you to develop.

Chapter 7

A Shoestring Summary

While it may be tempting to think that you should simply put together your project from scratch because your time is "free," remember that it actually comes with a cost. Paying for some of the tools, resources, or services highlighted in this chapter may help you develop your program more efficiently.

You may not be able to afford everything you'd like to bring into your next learning program. However, I've worked with many lean budgets as the training director in several nonprofit organizations, and there is often some funding available if you can make a business case.

Keep in mind that doing it all yourself can be a more expensive and lengthier option. Using limited budget resources strategically on tools, resources, or services can speed your development time and free you up to focus on other aspects, such as designing and developing the learning program or building relationships that are also essential for your success.

8
Paying for an Extra Set of Hands

I've spent most of my career as a training director responsible for internal training initiatives. I've often adopted the philosophy that either my team or I should do it all—the analysis, design, development, implementation, and evaluation of every project— especially in the beginning of my career. If I asked for funds for a contractor to take care of any of these steps, would people start to wonder what they were paying me for? Also, I worked mainly in nonprofit organizations, so I was always working on a shoestring.

My core competence is ILT, and I pride myself on the creativity I can bring to classroom training sessions. However, one of the best-designed and most effective projects I have ever worked on included funding for a contract instructional designer (SME) to help. This project needed to be completed during a particularly busy time when I was balancing several other major deliverables that could not be deprioritized. With the contract instructional designer's help, I suddenly had the capacity to deliver on everything.

In the past, I've asked the organization to purchase a license so I could to begin to learn how to use a rapid authoring tool, even though I knew there were people who specialized in e-learning development. While the projects I created were serviceable, they weren't nearly as good as the ones in which I had the funding to work with an e-learning developer. I still did all the storyboarding, but the e-learning developer I hired had much better visual design sense and could bring the project to life more quickly and beautifully than I could. Finding a freelance contractor or a firm specializing in e-learning development has multiplied my ability to get things done, with a more polished final product, because they've complemented my own skill set.

Chapter 8

Using an extra set of hands to help complete aspects of my instructional design projects is a lever that I've begun to appreciate. While I have about a million things I need to do every week, a contractor or vendor has one job: Focus on pushing forward the aspect of the project I've hired them to complete. I've found that paying for an extra set of hands helps projects move faster while freeing me to focus on other essential aspects of my job. That extra set of hands can sometimes shave *months* off the life cycle of a project.

Whether you currently have contractor funding or want to justify your request during the next budget season, this chapter will offer some ways to identify a vendor or contractor and insights into a few different areas where you may want to consider getting extra help during your next instructional design project.

Identifying the Right Vendor

If you have the funds, you can pay anyone to do anything. There are executive coaches, retreat facilitators, and strategic planners galore, but this chapter focuses on a handful of categories that are specific to instructional design, development, delivery, and evaluation.

Before we dive into each specialty area, let's review some broad questions you'll want to ask when determining whether to invest in an extra set of hands. And, if you're on a shoestring, these are especially important because you don't have time or money to waste on a poor vendor selection or bad fit for your project.

TIME SAVER
Previously Vetted or Approved Vendors

Does your company have a previously vetted or approved list of vendors? Ask your colleagues if they have worked with a vendor they liked. Certainly, do your own due diligence, but a recommendation from someone who has already worked with a vendor can provide insights that interview questions can't give you.

To identify the right vendor for your project, ask these questions:

- **Does the vendor need to understand your industry?** It may be tempting to seek out a vendor with experience in your industry, especially if the organization is involved in niche markets, because they may be able to offer additional subject matter expertise to your project. However, this could also be a disadvantage, as you may have a very specific way of doing things and don't want an outside vendor diluting your messaging or processes. If you have strong SMEs, whom you trust to provide the foundational content and will be available for your vendor to work with, then industry experience may be a lower priority.

- **What kind of working process or relationship do you want with the vendor?** If you're truly in a hurry, it may be tempting to hand over source materials to a vendor and have them return a finished product to you. While this may yield a rapidly developed final product, it may not always yield the final product you want. You'll have to choose whether to accept the imperfect, yet quickly developed product or spend more time making major revisions than if you had invested more time with the vendor up front. Some vendors will be comfortable taking your materials and turning around a final product, but others may prefer to forge a partnership with you that includes a slower development process and more check-ins along the way—this typically yields a final product closer to your ideal vision and fewer revisions.

- **What kind of experience does the vendor have with any technologies you require for your project?** If your new world-class e-learning module doesn't load smoothly into your LMS or uses more bandwidth than your learners have access to, then you and your vendor will find yourselves in a very frustrating spot. Specific technical requirements are just as important as content and learning design philosophy considerations.

- **Will you own (and be able to modify) all final assets provided by the vendor?** When one company my team worked with asked us this question, we were curious why they would ask. They told us that their previous vendor charged them each time they needed to print materials or visual aids for their ILT course. Another company we worked with said their previous e-learning vendor used a proprietary e-learning development tool, which meant all future updates needed to go through the vendor, and they charged an additional fee each time. Even if a vendor uses a widely available e-learning authoring tool, it doesn't mean that it's the same one your organization has a license for. You may also want to ask what software the vendor will use to create any print materials, such as facilitator or participant guides and handouts. Will they give you Word and PowerPoint files, or will they deliver a PDF? If they created the materials in a graphic design software your organization can't access, what will you do when you need to make changes?

- **How does the vendor define a successful project?** Sometimes, success is simply getting the project done on time and on budget. From a project management perspective, that's a perfect definition of success. From an instructional design standpoint, however, you may want to find out what your prospective extra set of hands understands about learning outcomes.

- **What happens if you're not completely satisfied with the product the vendor delivers?** Some vendors make as many changes as you need to be happy with the final product. Others limit the number of revisions, after which you'll pay for additional changes. Significant alterations or even simple requests after the original scope is agreed upon may also result in change orders and extra charges.

- **How do you know if the vendor can deliver the quality you need for your project?** Of course, you can ask all the questions you'd like, but some vendors will be able to interview well while others may not. One of the most important aspects of doing your due diligence will be to ask for work samples or a portfolio. When you review the portfolio, look for the types of activities you think might engage your audience, regardless of the subject matter represented in the portfolio. This may require some imagination on your part.

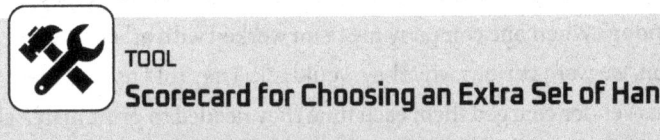

TOOL
Scorecard for Choosing an Extra Set of Hands

When putting all this together, having a scorecard may be helpful for you if you're comparing multiple vendors. Use or adapt the example in appendix A to evaluate vendors you're considering.

Where You May Need an Extra Set of Hands

The generic information and questions in the previous section can help you in a variety of situations. Now, we'll discuss several specialty areas to explore to help with your specific needs.

Full-Service Instructional Design

If you're running short on time—or you or your team has limited bandwidth because you're also trying to move 20 other projects forward—then you may need an extra set of hands to take your project from start to finish. This will be the most expensive option, but it could also be the most efficient way to move a learning initiative forward.

When contracting a full-service instructional design vendor, don't think you can just pay them to do your bidding, and then forget about the project until you receive the final deliverables. Even though you may be paying a vendor to move your learning initiative forward, you'll still need to connect them with your SMEs and review progress at various points to be sure everything is on track, the content is accurate, and the sequence and flow of the program aligns with your vision.

E-Learning Development

If you have a vision for the e-learning program—you know what content you want, what kinds of interactions you'd like to see, or how to put together an e-learning storyboard—but need some help bringing the module to life, then working with an e-learning developer may be a better option than trying to teach yourself basic (or advanced) e-learning development skills.

You have two options: Hire a solo freelancer or a company that specializes in e-learning development. A freelance e-learning developer might be all you need. They often have specialized skill sets in one (or more) popular authoring tools, an instructional design background or some experience, and might even be able to offer creative visual design. A firm that offers e-learning development may cost a little more, but it will also be able to allocate several people to the project who specialize in your e-learning authoring tool of choice, graphic design, editing, and quality control. This often ensures bugs are quickly identified and fixed before you receive the final deliverables.

Trainers and Facilitators

Sometimes, you're able to take an ILT project from start to finish by completing the actual instructional design, but you need an extra set of hands to deliver it. While an experienced facilitator should be able to pick up a set of well-crafted materials and deliver an effective learning experience, this is one area where industry knowledge can be quite helpful. You'll also want to consider a train-the-trainer program to help contracted trainers or facilitators become familiar with your content, materials, and activities. Allow them to ask questions and receive feedback to improve the effectiveness of their delivery in front of a live audience.

Learning Program Auditors and Evaluators

If your funding is tied to specific outcomes or training department performance metrics that require more than just reporting how many people attended or completed your training programs or what their average post-training satisfaction scores were, you may need to enlist some help with auditing your program for effectiveness and evaluating its results. Contractors who specialize in training program evaluation can be expensive, but they may be able to help you identify baseline metrics, data about how much of your training program is being transferred to the job, and measure the program's return on investment. If you go this route, be sure to bring the vendor into the instructional design process at the beginning of the project so that they can add value to your design from the start. Waiting until after you've designed and developed your program to come up with an evaluation plan means that you'll need to retrofit it to collect the most important data.

The softer the skill set your program focuses on, the more difficult it will be to identify and establish useful metrics. Also, keep in mind that no matter how much time and money you spend, it may be impossible to distinguish between the impact of your learning initiative and outside factors, such as organizational structure, the overall economy, and current market conditions.

Paying for an Extra Set of Hands

TIME SAVER
Creating an Effective RFP for an Instructional Design Vendor

Some organizations simply find a vendor they know and trust, discuss a new project, and then kick off the project with them. Other organizations need or prefer to go through a more formal request for proposal (RFP) process to identify the best vendor for the learning project.

The quality of responses you get from vendors will be directly related to the quality of your project description in the RFP. The less a vendor needs to guess what your needs are, the more specific and targeted their response should be. You'll also spend less time aligning needs and expectations once a vendor has been selected.

These details should be clear in any RFP your organization announces:
- Context and underlying project need
- What you believe success will look like a year after the project launches
- Information about the learners (such as how many, how they will digest the learning program, potential bandwidth issues, whether the program be accessed on phones, and if the information needs to be translated into other languages)
- Sound learning objectives based on instructional design principles
- Sample content or a link to content
- What time limits the will vendor need to work within (For ILT, is there a time limit? For e-learning, is there an expectation for module length?)
- Your preferred software or rapid authoring tool
- Expectations for how long development of the project should take
- Ideal timeframe for a project launch
- Contact information (and a deadline) to submit questions in advance of the proposal's due date

Chapter 8

A Shoestring Summary

Bringing in an outside vendor to help with some or all of your training program may help speed the project development time by months and increase your capacity to focus on other aspects of your job. Outside vendors will bring specific skill sets that you or your team may be lacking and serve as an extra set of hands. Like all other aspects of instructional design, it's important to analyze potential vendors, ask the right questions, and make sure that you end up paying the right partner for the work you need help with.

9
Paying for Off-the-Shelf Instructional Design Solutions

I worked on a project with a client who came to me during the peak of the pandemic and asked if I could help develop some virtual training for her company. As any good instructional designer should do, I told her that I was happy to help, but before I could start creating the training materials, I had a few questions. What exactly did she want to accomplish with training? Who was the audience? What were they lacking?

After going through a needs assessment and force ranking some different training topics, I thought we were ready to move forward with developing several training modules. As I began to think through what might go into the next statement of work, the COO turned to me and said, "Brian, I've had a conversation with the CEO. I told her that I have no doubt you could create an amazing set of training materials, but I'm not sure we need to go that far. I told her that because it seems like everyone needs different things, we can probably get what we need from LinkedIn Learning."

This was a small organization, and they certainly met the definition of operating on a shoestring. They had so much work and needed to upskill their staff quickly. They also had limited funds to invest in the training development. Once I set my ego aside, I realized that quick access to quality, ready-made, off-the-shelf training might be the best solution for them.

Off-the-shelf content refers to complete learning programs that are created by a third party. You pay for access—sometimes with a one-time or

129

Chapter 9

per-user fee and other times you're charged a licensing fee to use the content. Off-the-shelf content is available for both ILT and e-learning programs. When purchasing off-the-shelf content for ILT, you can either bring in a vendor to lead a prefabricated session or purchase materials from a vendor to facilitate yourself. Off-the-shelf e-learning content typically comes in several formats, including content that you can load into your own LMS for learners across your organization to access or paying to access content hosted by a third party's system.

In this chapter, we'll explore options for paying for off-the-shelf content when you're on a shoestring.

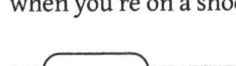 ON THE CHEAP
Saving Money for Individual Learning

There may be times when skills need to be developed or improved, but individual employees have very different needs from one another. A large-scale, one-topic-fits-all training program won't make sense in cases like this, but doing nothing isn't a good alternative. Giving specific individuals access to high quality, reputable, self-guided off-the-shelf content can be a much less expensive, and more effective, alternative.

Is an Off-the-Shelf Instructional Design Solution Right for You?

As I've mentioned earlier, the items in the "buy" part of this book are as close as you'll get to an easy button when it comes to instructional design. The work is mostly done for you, but it comes with a cost. If you're on a shoestring, the cost may not be ideal, but it doesn't mean you should avoid this approach. Here are some questions to consider when deciding if off-the-shelf instructional design is right for you:

- **What is your budget?** When you need to pay for something, this is the first question to ask. If you don't have a budget, then you can't buy things. But even if your budget is small, don't dismiss off-the-shelf instructional design as a possibility. Finding and paying for digital content providers (such as LinkedIn Learning or Skillsoft) may be more affordable than do-it-yourself solutions.

- **How niche is your content?** If you're looking for training on common topics—such as sales, marketing, soft skills, general leadership development, recruiting and retaining employees, or presentation skills—chances are that it's already been developed and is on sale now. You'll just need to scan through a variety of vendors to find the content that best fits your needs. Niche content—such as quality assurance in a highly regulated environment like a laboratory—may be less common, although some providers, including professional associations, may have what you're looking for. For highly specialized or confidential content, you'll either need to build it yourself or find a vendor to help you develop a custom program (with an NDA, of course).

- **How urgent is your need for a learning solution?** In any project, you can usually have two of three factors: price, quality, and speed. You can get a high-quality learning solution, fast, but it'll come with a cost. Or you can build a low-cost learning solution, but it may take weeks, months, or even years to complete. If you need a learning solution that has been well thought out, tried and tested, and run through a quality assurance cycle—quickly—an off-the-shelf solution may be your best answer.

- **Do you have other high-priority projects that need to be delivered?** When you have a bunch of priorities, then nothing is a priority, but that's too simplistic. If you need to deliver several high-priority projects, it's possible to accomplish everything, but you will need to prioritize where you devote your time and attention. Purchasing off-the-shelf content is one way that you may be able to do it all.

Pros and Cons of Buying Off-the-Shelf Content

Whether you're an instructional designer at an organization or you're a freelancer who contracts with organizations, purchasing off-the-shelf content is a solution worth exploring. Let's take a closer look at some of the pros and cons of this approach (Table 9-1).

Chapter 9

Table 9-1. Pros and Cons of Off-the-Shelf Content

Pros	• **So many choices!** With so many specialized vendors, a quick Google search will point you in the direction of content providers that can meet your individual and organizational needs— whether that's about leadership development, HR and hiring best practices, sales to USAID funding requirements, customer service, or coding basics. • **Ready immediately.** Once you've identified the needs of your learners or your organization, there is no design or development time. If you find the content you need, you can access it right away. • **Low effort.** Notice I didn't say no effort. While the content and materials have been created for you, you will still need to perform due diligence to be sure it meets your quality standards and your learners' needs. That said, you don't need to spend any time or effort (or take the time and effort of SMEs) to develop the learning program. • **Easily scalable.** Whether you purchase ILT or e-learning content, the plug and play materials can easily scale to learning experiences for large groups of learners. • **Costs that fit your budget.** Off-the-shelf content is available with several pricing models. Some high-end ILT or e-learning content may cost a lot of money, but there are also plenty of inexpensive solutions available for individuals or small groups.
Cons	• **More generic.** One of the biggest challenges with off-the-shelf content is that it needs to be specific enough to improve your knowledge or skills while also being generic enough to meet the needs and fit the contexts of different groups of people. For that reason, the content may be more generic than a learning program you create specifically for your organization. With off-the-shelf content, you'll also have limited (or no) opportunities for branding. • **Little or no control over content.** You may find that off-the-shelf content is almost perfect, except for one thing that doesn't apply to your company. Tough luck. In most cases, whether ILT or e-learning, what you see is what you get. Some vendors may offer customization for a price, but it's not usually an option. • **Updates are out of your hands.** For example, I delivered a cultural competence training program that featured an incredibly powerful video, but people have since pointed to the age of the video as a reason the whole training program seemed dated. We had not created the training program or the specific video, so we had no control over updates to the materials. When selecting off-the-shelf programs, you may be able to ask a vendor about the frequency of updates to the content, but they will generally be out of your hands.

Table 9-1. Pros and Cons of Off-the-Shelf Content (Cont.)

- **Quality may vary.** Not all off-the-shelf content is created equal. While I've identified "costs that fit your budget" as a pro, you also need to adopt a "buyer beware" philosophy: You will often get what you pay for. Read through the materials before making a final purchasing decision so you can verify that the quality of the content and production value of the materials are to your satisfaction.
- **Some pricing models.** Some off-the-shelf content, particularly the high-end programs, may require long-term usage commitments or come with strange licensing requirements. Read the fine print on the pricing and licensing models to be sure you don't get roped into an agreement that's not as good of a deal as creating a program on your own.

Keep in mind that thinking, "If you build it, they will come," doesn't necessarily mean people will be clamoring to attend or complete the most creative and useful training program you can develop. So, "If you buy it, they will come," also doesn't guarantee people will want to complete any off-the-shelf content you make available. In fact, I worked for an organization that purchased a library of more than 100 e-learning courses and made them available for all staff, but a year after the purchase, fewer than 5 percent of staff had completed a single course.

Off-the-shelf content offers a shortcut through the design and development pieces of your instructional design process, but it does not exempt you from analysis, implementation, or evaluation. So, while you may *buy* the actual course, you may still need to invest time *building* your learning ecosystem (See chapter 4).

TOOL
Off-the-Shelf Rapid Decision-Making Survey

Whenever you're faced with a decision between buying off-the-shelf content and building it yourself, use the rapid decision-making survey in appendix A to help choose the best path forward.

Chapter 9

Sources of Off-the-Shelf Content

Off-the-shelf instructor-led training content can be found in several places, including:

- **Trade associations.** If you're looking for a course on training design (or anything related to training and talent development), the Association for Talent Development has an entire catalog of courses available. If you work in the transportation sector, you can find anything from retail tire store leadership to tire technician training materials through the Tire Industry Association. If you need to prepare your eye recovery technicians for the Certified Eye Bank Technician exam (because you lead training initiatives for an eye bank but don't have the time or technical expertise to develop a review course), then the Eye Bank Association of America has you covered. Many trade associations offer core instruction and coursework in both in-person and virtual formats. Some offer e-learning modules as well.

- **Professional collectives.** One of the best training sessions I've ever experienced was designed and facilitated by a group of human resources attorneys in Seattle, Washington, who came to our office and trained 25 of our people managers on adopting a more consistent hiring process. There are many nonprofit and for-profit collectives of specialized professionals who have found their niche in designing training for specific aspects of any business.

- **Specialty companies.** There are also many experienced individuals and boutique firms that specialize in developing training courses on topics ranging from fraud prevention to customer service to new manager training to safety and compliance, and everything in between. Some courses are structured so that people from your company can attend as part of a cohort with individuals from other organizations. Some training design companies will deliver a workshop (at your office or virtually) to a group of your employees. Other companies also provide prefabricated curricula or instructional videos with facilitation guides for you to purchase and deliver on your own.

For digital off-the-shelf learning experiences, there are several sources you may want to explore, including:

Paying for Off-the-Shelf Instructional Design Solutions

- **Learning content providers.** If you're looking for self-directed, off-the-shelf digital content, the internet has no shortage of providers offering courses on nearly any topic you can imagine. The most well-known and reputable sites for these modules include LinkedIn Learning, Udemy, Skillsoft, and Coursera. Some content can be accessed through the provider's site using individual logins, or it may also be purchased (or licensed) and loaded onto your organization's LMS.
- **Specialty companies.** Like with ILT content, there are also specialty companies that offer e-learning modules or other digital content that can range from high-level, generic topic overviews to niche and specialized information and skill-building experiences. If you're wiling to pay a premium, you may have more flexibility when working with a specialty company to apply branding, update content, and request organization-specific modifications.

A Shoestring Summary

Once you've decided that training is the best solution to help increase knowledge or build skills, you then need to decide whether you (or your team) are the best resource to design and develop the learning experience. Off-the-shelf content may be a more cost-effective, time sensitive way to offer training on a variety of topics to your organization. However, while buying off-the-shelf content speeds you past the design and development phases of ADDIE, you still need to analyze potential solutions offered by different vendors. You'll also need to give additional time and attention to the implementation and evaluation of projects that use off-the-shelf solutions.

135

Bringing It All Together

In the first part of this book, I walked you through strategies for building your instructional design project. The second part focused on ways to borrow time and inspiration from others. The third part introduced a variety of tools, services, and resources you can buy to help push your instructional design forward. Now, let's put all these concepts together.

While I've written about what it means to build, borrow, and buy, this book wouldn't be complete unless I shared some thoughts on when you might want to build, borrow, or buy. There are two main factors that people typically point to when working on a shoestring: running short on money and running out of time.

When You're Short on Money

Figure 10-1 offers a visual idea of what you may need to do when you're limited on the amount of money you have available for your instructional design project.

Figure 10-1. Building, Borrowing, or Buying With Limited Money

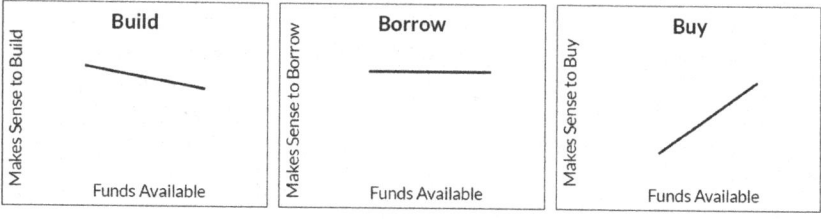

With less money, you will need to build more of your project from scratch, but that doesn't mean you have to build it exclusively from scratch. Borrowing should be part of your instructional design process, and even with limited funds,

Bringing It All Together

you can buy low-cost tools, resources, or services to make your instructional design process easier or better. (Obviously, the more funds available, the more the *buy* option can be part of your strategy.)

Let's review several variations of a limited funds scenario through the build-borrow-buy framework. Read through the scenarios in this chapter and jot down some notes using the ADDIE Build-Borrow-Buy Matrix in appendix A to see what you might do in this situation. Then, turn to my completed examples in appendix B to compare your thoughts with mine.

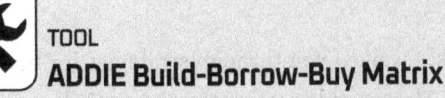

TOOL
ADDIE Build-Borrow-Buy Matrix

Use the matrix in appendix A to outline your thoughts based on what you've read in this book and your own previous experiences. To help you get started, I've filled in the first row.

	Build	**Borrow**	**Buy**
Analysis	• Identify success metrics for new product launch, user adoption, and customer support.	• Do a quick Google search for similar tools and how other companies offer new user support and onboarding. (Maybe sign up for a free trial to experience new user onboarding.)	• With no funds available, I'd make notes of every aspect of this project and how it could be more effective and efficient, such as purchasing screencast software that offers advanced features and opportunities for branding.
Design			
Develop			
Implement			
Evaluate			

138

Bringing It All Together

Scenario 1. New User Onboarding at Your Tech Start-Up

You just began working for a tech start-up that is ready to launch a new product. As part of the launch, you need to put together an on-demand, new user onboarding program that will serve as a self-service portal for new users to learn about important product features, as well as a quick reference guide for users attempting to navigate advanced features of the system. Your supervisor says, "I need you to embrace the start-up mentality. There might be some money available down the road to make this program look more professional, but for now, you'll have to be creative. I'm sure you'll come up with something good!"

Scenario 2. Competing Medium-Priority Compliance Training Projects

You look at all the sticky notes around your desk and your heart sinks. Each one represents a to-do list for a separate project. You have a bunch of medium-priority compliance training projects that you've promised to create for your supervisor, but they never get done. You have a license to an industry-leading rapid e-learning authoring tool, but you know other people could make much better e-learning modules. You don't have any budget for these training projects, but you need complete them. It might be time to embrace the idea that although they may not turn out pretty or slick, they'll be good enough if created with sound instructional design practices.

When You're Short on Time

If you examine Figure 10-2 closely, you'll notice these graphs look different than the ones in Figure 10-1—the less time you have, the less sense it makes for you to build something from scratch. Yes, it always makes sense to *borrow*, but when you have less time available, you should consider the benefits of buying some or all of your instructional design solution.

Figure 10-2. Building, Borrowing, or Buying With Limited Time

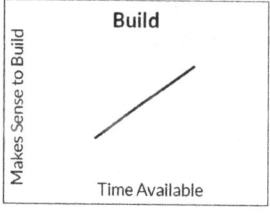 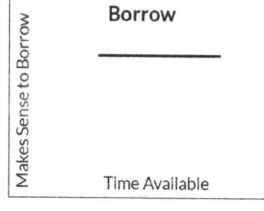 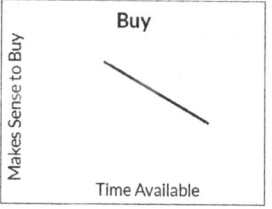

139

Bringing It All Together

Let's review a third scenario in which limited time affects your instructional design process.

Scenario 3. Multiday Training Across 16 Offices Within Two Months

You have funding to create a two-day training session that will be delivered in 16 offices across the country over the next two months. The project needs to be launched—with facilitator and participant materials designed, developed, tested for quality, and ready to go—two months from today. The project sponsor will also want to see some initial results from the program once it's live. It would be nice if this was the only thing on your to-do list, but you have other (lower priority) projects, as well as the continued support and supervision of your three employees.

When You're Short on Time and Money

Wouldn't it be nice if you were only ever short on either time or money? Unfortunately, life doesn't work like that, and there will be times when you're short on both. What's an instructional designer to do in those situations? Let's review one final scenario.

Scenario 4. Support 20 New Product Launches Over the Next Year

The sales reps across your organization need information about new products a week before they are launched for the general public. Over the next year, you're told that 20 new products are being launched, and you're the one responsible for making sure the sales reps are prepared a week in advance of each launch. Some products are just updates of older products, so sales reps won't need in-depth knowledge about them. However, other products will be completely new, so sales reps will need detailed information about them. While there are other trainers in your organization, you're a department of one. You have access to several authoring tools and an organization-wide LMS but no additional funds for these projects. You'll typically receive the information about each new product two weeks prior to its launch.

Compare Your Answers With Mine

Turn to appendix B to compare your thoughts with mine. Remember that each scenario's one paragraph description leaves a lot of room for interpretation. Your background and experiences may differ quite a lot from mine, so you may imagine them very differently. There is no one right way to address any of these scenarios, but I hope you'll find value in thinking them through and then comparing your thoughts with mine.

What's Next?

As you can see, there is no one specific formula to follow when engaging in instructional design on a shoestring. It will look different depending on whether you have any funds available or you're pressed for time. It will look different depending on the expectations for your final product and your vision, which may be based upon other experiences you've had.

Good instructional design on a shoestring requires some structure, flexibility, creativity, and quick thinking. You may borrow others' time; study examples that have come before you; use tools, resources, or services that make things a little easier; and accept that even if you don't have a ton of time or access to a lot of money, you can still produce an effective learning experience based on sound educational theory and adult learning principles.

This is the kind of stuff that miracles are made of.

APPENDIX A
TOOLS AND TEMPLATES

Visit endurancelearning.com/books/shoestring to download printable versions of these templates:

- Putting ADDIE to Work
- Quiz: How Ruthless Are You?
- Lesson Plan for Instructor-Led Training
- Facilitator Guide
- E-Learning Storyboard
- Informal Learning Options
- Increasing the Potential for Success
- Subject Matter Expert Qualification Sheet
- Low-Lift Strategies to Involve Supervisors
- Ensuring You Get the Feedback You Need
- Options for Paying for Convenience
- Scorecard for Choosing an Extra Set of Hands
- Off-the-Shelf Rapid Decision-Making Survey
- ADDIE Build-Borrow-Buy Matrix

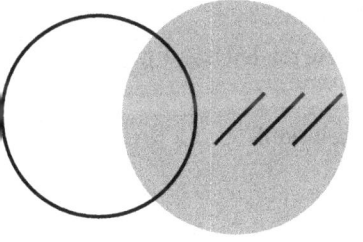

Appendix A

Putting ADDIE to Work

If you want to test how using a structure like the ADDIE model can help your program (or could have helped you with a past project), try answering these questions for yourself.

Analyze:
- What problem do we want to solve? Or, what opportunity can we build on?
- How do we know it's a problem (or opportunity)?
- What would happen if we did nothing?
- What do we know about the target audience?
- If training is part of the solution, what barriers could we encounter?
- What needs to change based upon this learning initiative, and how will we know if this happens? How will success be defined and measured for this initiative?
- What is the timeline for this project?
- Who and where will the content come from?

Before you move on to design	Yes	No
Do you have a clear business or performance need?		
Will a learning or training program solve the problem?		
Have you defined what "success" will look like?		
Do you know enough about the audience, timeline, and need?		

Design:
- How will stakeholders (SMEs, project sponsors, and so on) be engaged?
- What should people be able to do differently or better?
- Is the ultimate outcome awareness or skill development, or is it non-learning-related (such as team building)?
- What success metrics will be evaluated, and how will that information be collected?
- Is the design inclusive of all learners?
- What is the best way to get the learners what they need?
- Who will deliver the session (if we design an instructor-led training program)?
- Where will this live (if we design an e-learning solution)?

144

Appendix A

Before you move on to development	Yes	No
Have you determined the best structure for this project? (Will it be a one-off event, job aid, or a mixture of formal training program and informal learning resources?)		
Are there unique design considerations (such as inclusivity or accessibility) that need to be considered during development?		
Have you clearly outlined your evaluation strategies?		
Has the project sponsor signed off on the design?		

Develop:
- Who will be involved in the development?
- What quality assurance (QA) measures or processes do we need?
- When will the project's development be deemed complete?

Before you move on to implementation	Yes	No
Have you checked for errors, including big showstoppers (such as incorrect content, e-learning buttons that don't work, slides that don't advance, or incorrect logo placement) and small typos and grammar mistakes?		
Will the people who facilitate, distribute, or communicate about this project know how to use the materials and how to interact with the intended audience?		

Implement:
- How will the final files be turned over to key stakeholders?
- How will facilitators be prepared to deliver the program (if we design an instructor-led training program)?

Before you move on to evaluation	Yes	No
Are there changes, adjustments, or areas that need to be overhauled based on the learning solution's initial implementation?		

Evaluate:
- Did the program do what we intended? How do we know?

145

Appendix A

Quiz: How Ruthless Are You?

Using a 10-point scale, rate how comfortable you would be in each of the following situations. Score a 1 if you hate the idea being described or if it makes you extremely uncomfortable; a 10 if you love the idea or wouldn't hesitate for a moment.

Then, total your score and chart it on the line below to see where you fall on the Ruthless Spectrum.

Questions	Scale 1–10
If someone tells me that I need to cut my learning experience down from 90 minutes to 60 minutes, my first instinct is to welcome the opportunity to make a leaner learning experience.	
I can easily explain the difference between *my goals* (or a *SME's goals*) and the *learning objectives* for a learning experience.	
I consistently and intentionally connect every activity in a learning experience with a learning objective.	
I'm comfortable saying no to someone else's idea.	
I know the difference between information that I find *interesting* and information that is *essential* for helping someone learn how to do something new, different, or better.	
I can evaluate my own lesson plans or storyboards and easily cut something out, even when I'm emotionally invested in the idea and a piece of me might die seeing that idea on the cutting room floor.	
Total Score	

0
Big old softie
"I know we need to
prioritize, but seriously,
everything on this topic is
both unique and
important."

60
Ice in your veins
"Just tell me what the
goals are and how much
time we have, and there
will be no dilly dallying."

Appendix A

Lesson Plan for Instructor-Led Training

I've shared this lesson plan template with thousands of people to help them better organize their learning experience in alignment with sound instructional design practices.

Lesson Plan for Instructor-Led Training		
Training segment title:		
Training segment goal:		
Date and time:		
Learning objectives:		
By the end of this training segment, the participants will be able to:		
Materials:		
Estimated Time	**Content and Key Points**	**Instructional Technique:**

147

Appendix A

Facilitator Guide

My colleagues and I have used this facilitator guide template for many projects.

Estimated time for this segment	Topic or Training Segment

Slide thumbnail #1 of material to be covered	Step-by-step instructions and talking points:

Slide thumbnail #1 of material to be covered

Slide thumbnail #2 of material to be covered

List of materials needed for this topic or segment:

- Flipchart
- Markers
- Handouts or participant guide page references
- Sticky notes
- Voting dots

Step-by-step instructions and talking points:

1. Introduction to topic or segment
2. Anchor activity instructions
3. Content talking point 1
4. Content talking point 2
5. Application activity
6. Application activity debrief questions
7. Resources or materials for future use
8. Call to action
9. Transition to next topic or segment

Appendix A

E-Learning Storyboard

This storyboard template can not only help keep your thoughts organized before you bring the content to life in the e-learning authoring tool, but it can also help keep everyone involved in the project (including SMEs, the e-learning developer, and key stakeholders who need to review the content) on the same page. Use this storyboard to map your thoughts and get the approval of reviewers about the sequence, flow, and content prior to building your e-learning module. Doing this can save you both time and money on an e-learning project.

Title of E-Learning Module			
Objectives: By the end of the month, learners will be able to: 1. 2. 3. 4. 5.			
ID	**Screen Text**	**Developer Notes**	**Voice-Over**

Appendix A

Informal Learning Options

If you can address a learning need without requiring people to take time away from their work to attend a training session or complete an e-learning course, then perhaps one (or a combination of several) of these informal options may be a better solution:

- Bulleted list
- Checklist
- List of steps or procedures
- Flowchart
- Illustrated guide
- Cheat sheet
- Quick reference guide
- Rubric
- Evaluation form or template
- Data table
- Automated wizard
- Decision tree
- Pros and cons list
- Script
- FAQ document
- Microlearning
- Video tutorial
- Introduction video
- Explainer video
- Long-form video
- Stretch assignment or hands-on work
- Drip campaign
- Chatbot or AI solution

Appendix A

Increasing the Potential for Success

Use this worksheet to identify potential barriers to your program's success and how you may address each one.

Barrier	How will you address it?	Who can you work with to address it?
Learners don't think they have time.		
Learners revert to old habits.		
Learners forget what they learned.		
Learners don't know how to apply what they've learned.		
Learners don't have the necessary access to technology or resources.		
Supervisors are ambivalent or unengaged.		
Supervisors are actively against the learning program.		

Appendix A

Subject Matter Expert Qualification Sheet

If you have any say in the SME you'll be working with, use this SME qualification sheet, developed by my colleague Heather Barry, to help find the right person.

Quality	Yes	No	Clarifying Question
Deep content understanding			Is this person a jack of all trades or a master of one? SMEs should be a master of their domain.
Unique experience or perspective			Does this person have any experience with the subject that is unlike others familiar with the content?
Demonstrated willingness to share			SMEs spend a lot of time learning everything about their subject. A good SME has a history of sharing their information by writing help documents or coaching others.
Available			SMEs tend to be busy, especially if training is related to a release or initiative. Is this person available during all review periods, even if the timelines are extended?
Training ambassador			Does this person believe in the training that is being developed?
Cross domain understanding			Do they simply know how something works or do they truly understand how the information interacts with other information?
Project specific quality			

©2018 Endurance Learning

Appendix A

Low-Lift Strategies to Involve Supervisors

While you don't need to do every strategy each time you develop a learning initiative, using one or a combination of strategies can help your learners' supervisors help you increase the likelihood that learning will be transferred to the job. These items can be shared as handouts during instructor-led training programs or downloads in an e-learning module.

Checklist: Low-Lift Strategies to Involve Supervisors in Your Learning Initiative	
❑	Goal-setting form for supervisor to review with learner
❑	Questions for a supervisor to ask learners to help them set goals
❑	Self-evaluation form (for learners) to compare with supervisor's evaluation form
❑	Rubric that specifically outlines what exceptional, adequate, and below adequate performance looks like when using new information or skills
❑	Action plan with specific actions to be taken by certain deadlines

153

Appendix A

Ensuring You Get the Feedback You Need

The following is an email by my colleague Lauren Wescott sent to a client when it was time for them to review the first draft of an e-learning module. I've removed some details and made it more generic, but you can use it as a template the next time you're looking for feedback on a learning initiative.

Hello review team,

It's time to get this party officially started! What we have ready for you today is the first outline of the e-learning module for this initiative. We are ready for you four to complete an outline review.

A few notes about this outline:
- Outlines are broad sweeping documents. The point is to begin to come together on sequence, flow, content, and possible interaction ideas.
- It can be a bit difficult to get a feel for things, especially from these outlines as they are, quite frankly, entirely unremarkable and lack the fun visuals and things that will ultimately bring these modules to life.
- The ideas in the outline in no way represent the full extent of the module, wording, or content, but instead exist as a skeletal structure for us to come together and agree upon as we look to build out from here.

What we need from you:
- Please review this outline and provide your thoughts and feedback using Track Changes and comments in Word.
- Project leads, I will trust that you will coordinate the feedback among the four of you on your end! (Please don't leave competing or conflicting comments in the margins; we won't know which direction to move forward.) :)
- As you review, consider:
  ◦ What's missing? Have we not included something that is essential?
  ◦ Is there more of an emphasis on something that you wish there was less emphasis on?
  ◦ Is there an interaction idea that just doesn't spark your fancy? Please let us know.
  ◦ Please, please throw in your own ideas and aspirations for these modules as you review!
- With our powers combined, we will land on something greater in the end!
- At this point, your feedback is incredibly valuable to us! While we will work on trying to craft the best learning experiences, you ultimately know the content best, and we highly value your ideas and input as we begin to dive in together. You also won't hurt our feelings if you think we've done something absolutely absurd here! It's totally the correct time to chime in and let us know if it appears we are heading in the wrong direction.

Appendix A

We would appreciate your combined feedback on this outline by Tuesday, February 14.

Overview of next steps:

1. **Outline review:** (This is where we are now.) Review the outline document for sequence and flow. Note anything that appears to be missing or has too much emphasis. Think of this as the skeletal system of the module. We need to make sure we have all the correct bones in place.

2. **Script review:** After we receive your feedback on the outline, we will jump into scripting. The script will be for the whole module, including onscreen text, interactions, and voice-over text. This is when we will really count on you four to provide us with the in-depth feedback on the content, interactions, and wording choices. This is likely the point when your reviews will be the most important (and likely time consuming), as we look to craft the best module possible.

3. **Module review:** We will incorporate your feedback and then send the module to development. This is when we will build everything out. This is also when you will see the module itself in all its glory! There will be an AI voice-over in place during your review, as we solidify the wording is exactly as it should be. This is the point at which we once again lean on the four of you to clarify any wording changes necessary before we send the module to voice-over.

4. **Final module review:** This is when you will see the clean and shiny module with the real voice-over and closed captions and accessibility in place and tightened up. The module will also have received thorough quality assurance testing prior to this final review. You will review the module, note any issues, and give final approval. Then, we send over SCORM and you get to launch these to the world!

Each of these steps will happen for all modules in this series, and we will likely have mul-tiple things happening at once (such as script review on one module, outline review on an-other, and development and module review on yet another). We will work to balance your review loads so that you do not have an overwhelming amount of reviews on your plate, and our general rule is to ask you to complete a review cycle in five working days. However, please let us know if at any point we need to adjust our schedules or allow for additional review time during this process.

That's it for now. Please let me know if you have any questions as you dive in and begin this process! We're excited to get this course rolling along!

Lauren Wescott
Learning and Development Manager
Endurance Learning

Appendix A

Options for Paying for Convenience

Check out this list of web-based applications you can use to make your learning program more effective and engaging for your learners and easier for you to develop:

- **Quiz, gaming, and survey platforms**
  - Mentimeter
  - Poll Everywhere
  - Kahoot
  - Quizizz
  - Quizlet
  - Google Surveys
  - Microsoft Forms
  - SurveyMonkey
- **Rapid authoring tools**
  - Articulate Storyline
  - Articulate Rise
  - Adobe Captivate
  - Lectora
  - dominKnow One
  - isEazy
- **Visual design software**
  - Microsoft PowerPoint
  - Adobe InDesign
  - Adobe Photoshop
  - Canva
  - Pixlr
- **Animation software**
  - Vyond
  - PowToon

Appendix A

Scorecard for Choosing an Extra Set of Hands

Having a scorecard may be helpful if you're comparing multiple vendors. You can use this example to evaluate vendors you're considering or adapt it to your needs.

For each category, assign a score of 1 (worst possible response) to 10 (best possible response). You may wish to use a multiplier for categories that are more important than others when evaluating prospective vendors.

Criteria	Vendor 1	Vendor 2	Vendor 3
Understands our industry			
Process and working relationship			
Experience with our technologies and requirements			
Flexibility of final deliverables and assets			
Definition of "success"			
Process for making it right			
Experience and portfolio			
Total			
Notes			

Appendix A

Off-the-Shelf Rapid Decision-Making Survey

Whenever you're faced with a decision to buy off-the-shelf content or to build it yourself, pull out this rapid decision-making survey. If you answer yes more than no, you may want to consider using an off-the-shelf solution.

Yes	No	Survey Questions
❑	❑	Do you have or can you ask for budget?
❑	❑	Is your content generic?
❑	❑	Is the need for your learning program urgent?
❑	❑	Do you have other high-priority projects that need to be delivered?
❑	❑	Do you have time to evaluate and vet your choices?
❑	❑	Do you need to scale the experience to a large group of learners?
❑	❑	Are there opportunities to integrate the content into other learning experiences?
❑	❑	Does your company already have an off-the-shelf vendor you can turn to for this need?

Appendix A

ADDIE Build-Borrow-Buy Matrix

Use this matrix at the start of your next instructional design project to brainstorm possible solutions that fit the available time, budget, and resources.

	Build	Borrow	Buy
Analysis			
Design			
Develop			
Implement			
Evaluate			

APPENDIX B
WORKED EXAMPLES

Review the four scenarios introduced in "Bringing It All Together" and use the ADDIE Build-Borrow-Buy Matrix to collect your ideas. Think about what you've read in this book, as well as your own experiences. As you compare your thoughts with mine, remember that the one paragraph description of each scenario leaves a lot of room for interpretation. Your background and experiences may differ quite a lot from mine, so you may imagine it very differently. There is no one right way to address any of these scenarios, but I hope you'll find value in thinking them through and then comparing your thoughts with mine.

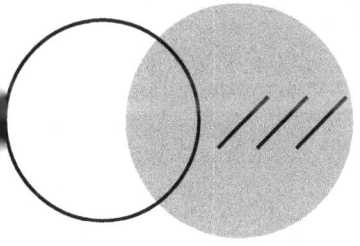

Scenario 1. New User Onboarding at Your Tech Start-Up

	Build	Borrow	Buy
Analysis	• Identify success metrics for new product launch, user adoption, and customer support. • Spend time understanding the users, including how and when they will use the product and whether in-the-flow-of-work performance support may be needed. • Speak with SMEs and users, if possible, to understand exactly what content users will need and where they may need the most support.	• Do a quick Google search for similar tools to see how other companies offer new user support and onboarding. (Maybe sign up for a free trial to experience new user onboarding.) • Borrow time from SMEs and possibly users.	• While there aren't funds currently available, I'd make notes of every aspect of this project and how it could be more effective and efficient, such as purchasing screencast software that offers advanced features and opportunities for branding.
Design	• Develop an FAQ. • Create a checklist of key functions and navigational paths that must be executed for data to be useful and clean. • Create a new user onboarding map that shows each step of the onboarding process and allows a user to track where they are and how much time remains.	• Research maps from shopping malls and other locations that include a "you are here" label. Break down the components of the maps and why they're for users. Identify transferable lessons to help new users navigate the software.	

Develop	• Write a series of video tutorials, based on SME (and possibly user) interviews, that walk new users through common features and navigational paths. • Refine the professional look of any documentation being released, including the FAQ, checklist, and map. • Use a free, online screencast recording software to record screenshots, screen navigation, and voice-overs.	• Work with the communications team to ensure that new users are informed about the new user onboarding and support portal once it goes live.
Implement	• Launch a portal with the FAQ, checklist, map, and screencasts.	
Evaluate		• Ask for support with monitoring new user adoption rates, and ask for feedback on where new users get stuck and whether the initial materials are helpful.

Scenario 2. Competing Medium-Priority Compliance Training Projects

	Build	Borrow	Buy
Analysis	• Look past the stomach-turning label of "compliance training," and identify why these courses are necessary and how each should differ due to the content. • Determine whether every staff member needs to complete every course every year, whether once covers them for life, or whether they can test out of any courses. • Review existing materials and define learning objectives for each course. • Determine how course completion will be documented. Determine whether additional metrics beyond course completion will be necessary. • Prioritize courses to be completed, and establish a timeline, including a review of materials by appropriate stakeholders. • Absent strong support for that idea, I may want to invest in customized stock imagery to tell a more refined visual story in each module.		• If better visual design can make these modules more effective through better engagement and a more professional look and feel, I may need to make the case that these modules should eventually be revised and refined by a professional e-learning developer or graphic designer.

Design	Create storyboards for each compliance module using the anchor-content-application-future use model: ◦ Anchor activity ◦ Compliance content ◦ Application ◦ Final question for reflection • Coordinate with HR to engage employees prior to launch (to garner awareness about the modules) and after the launch (to follow up and hold employees accountable for completion).	• Conduct a Google search of similar compliance topics to see how others have presented this information. • Review the E-Learning Heroes website to see if you can download any partial courses or templates that align with these compliance topics.
Develop	• Use a rapid authoring tool to bring the storyboard to life.	• Use pixabay.com for imagery.
Implement	• Launch modules.	
Evaluate	• Work with HR to monitor completion and compliance metrics.	

Scenario 3. Multiday Training Across 16 Offices Within Two Months

	Build	Borrow	Buy
Analysis	• Identify success metrics and learning objectives for the program, and determine the sequence and flow of content. Also define what would be out of scope for this project. • Talk with representatives from each of the regional offices to determine if a one-size-fits-all approach is appropriate, or if some offices need to focus on certain areas or will push back on certain topics. • Decide how in-person delivery will be done, and by whom.	• Identify champions at each regional office who can generate enthusiasm and spread the word about this program.	• Identify an instructional design vendor to support this project.
Design	• Coordinate between the SMEs, instructional design vendor, and other stakeholders to review and approve draft materials.		• Identify contract trainers who can go through a train-the-trainer program and deliver the two-day sessions. • Work with the instructional design vendor to create lesson plans and final materials that include:

Develop		○ A lesson plan for a kickoff virtual session to introduce all 16 offices to the program and set the expectations for the in-person, on-site component ○ A train-the-trainer session for contract trainers ○ A lesson plan for the two-day program
	• Review materials from vendor. • Coordinate schedule with contract trainers.	• Instructional design vendor will produce final, polished materials.
Implement	• Attend train-the-trainer and select pilot versions of the two-day program; then work with the vendor on any requested changes.	• Communicate with supervisors on how they can support this initiative.	• Conduct a train-the-trainer program. • Contract trainers to facilitate sessions at regional offices.
Evaluate	• Review Level 1 feedback, and prepare for a future project that will include Level 3 feedback.	• Follow up with supervisors and learners.	• Contract trainers to facilitate Level 1 feedback.

Scenario 4. Support 20 New Product Launches Over the Next Year

	Build	Borrow	Buy
Analysis	• Talk with sales reps to determine if formal, informal, or a combination of both learning solution types would be most appropriate to support product launches. • Collect information to develop a calendar for product launches. • Identify specific products and the learning objectives for each product launch support component. • Identify sales metrics for determining if these resources lead to better results.	• Connect with other trainers across the organization to understand what they do to support their teams and what transferable lessons I can take from them.	• Nothing will be purchased during this initiative; however, I will keep an eye on emerging technologies and best practices and collect ideas so that I'm prepared if a business case can be made to provide better or more efficient product launch support in the future.
Design	• Depending on the product launch and whether it will require a light or heavy touch: 　◦ Develop a product FAQ (for all). 　◦ Create a "what's new" document (for updated products). 　◦ Storyboard a video script for new product developers to talk about the new products. 　◦ Develop several sales scenarios to serve as a final assessment (for all).	• Review tutorials for creating effective videos for learning from a YouTube channel hosted by several conference speakers who spoke at last year's ATD International Conference & Exposition.	

Develop	• Publish FAQ and "what's new" documents. • Use a virtual conference platform to record product developers, and then use video editing software to ensure learners only see necessary components. • Use a rapid e-learning authoring tool to bring sales scenarios to life.	• Schedule time for product developer videos.	
Implement	• Notify sales reps that resources are available no later than seven days in advance of a new product launch.		
Evaluate		• Work with the operations team to access sales metrics; comparing data from people who have completed coursework or used resources with those who haven't.	

References and Resources

Allen, M., and R. Sites. 2012. *Leaving ADDIE for SAM: An Agile Model for Developing the Best Learning Experiences.* Alexandria, VA: ATD Press.

Broad, M.L., and J.W. Newstrom. 1992. *Transfer of Training: Action-Packed Strategies to Ensure High Payoff From Training Investment.* New York: Basic Books.

Brown, P.C., H.L. Roediger III, and M.A. McDaniel. 2014. *Make It Stick: The Science of Successful Learning.* Boston, MA: Harvard University Press.

Center for Creative Leadership. 2022. "The 70-20-10 Rule for Leadership Development." Leading Effectively, April 24. ccl.org/articles /leading-effectively-articles/70-20-10-rule.

Clark, R.C., and R.E. Mayer. 2016. *E-Learning and the Science of Instruction: Proven Guidelines for Consumers and Designers of Multimedia Learning,* 4th ed. Hoboken, NJ: John Wiley and Sons.

Dirksen, J. 2016. *Design for How People Learn,* 2nd ed. San Francisco: New Riders.

Google. n.d. "Arts & Culture." artsandculture.google.com.

Green, A. 2022. "ADDIE: The Origin of Modern-Day ISD" Ch. 11 in *ATD's Handbook for Training and Talent Development,* edited by Elaine Biech. Alexandria, VA: ATD Press.

Hodell, C. 2015. *ISD from the Ground Up: A No-Nonsense Approach to Instructional Design,* 4th ed. Alexandria, VA: ATD Press.

Jain, A. 2021. "5 Key Principles for Designing and Delivering Video-Based Learning." ATD Webinar. April 6. webcasts.td.org/webinar/4025.

Jones, K., and J. Lumsden. 2023. *Needs Assessment on a Shoestring.* Alexandria, VA: ATD Press.

References and Resources

Kapp, K., and R. Defelice. 2019. *Microlearning: Short and Sweet.* Alexandria, VA: ATD Press.

Kapp, K., and R. Defelice. 2022. "Microlearning Basics." Podcast. *Train Like You Listen,* July 18. endurancelearning.com/blog/microlearning-basics.

Kapp, K.M. 2012. *The Gamification of Learning and Instruction: Game-Based Methods and Strategies for Training and Education.* San Francisco: Pfeiffer.

Kotter, J. 1995. "Leading Change: Why Transformation Efforts Fail." *Harvard Business Review,* May. hbr.org/1995/05/leading-change-why-transformation -efforts-fail-2.

Kotter, J., and H. Rathgeber. 2006. *Our Iceberg Is Melting: Changing and Succeeding Under Any Conditions.* New York: St. Martin's Press.

Kotter, J.P., and D.S. Cohen. 2002. *The Heart of Change: Real-life Stories of How People Change Their Organizations.* Boston, MA: Harvard Business Review Press.

Margol, E. 2017. "Microlearning to Boost the Employee Experience." *TD at Work.* Alexandria, VA: ATD Press.

McGonigal, J. 2011. *Reality Is Broken: Why Games Make Us Better and How They Can Change the World.* New York: Penguin.

Museum Environments. n.d. "Planning the Museum Experience." museum environments.com/museumexperience.

Pierce, M. 2022. "Your Year for Video! Getting Started, Leveling Up, and Making Better Videos." Video. The Visual Lounge, January 13. youtube.com/watch ?v=QQi6NdW1P_A.

Thalheimer, W. 2006. *Spacing Learning Events Over Time: What the Research Says.* Somerville, MA: Work-Learning Research. worklearning.com/wp-content /uploads/2017/10/Spacing_Learning_Over_Time_March2009v1_.pdf.

Thalheimer, W. 2015. "Learning Objectives—A Research-Inspired Odyssey." Video. Work-Learning Research, January 29. youtu.be/PRX1RwxybCs.

Torgerson, C., and S. Iannone. 2019. *Designing Microlearning.* Alexandria, VA: ATD Press.

Torrance, M. 2019. *AGILE for Instructional Designers: Iterative Project Management to Achieve Results.* Alexandria, VA: ATD Press.

Torrance, M., and R. Houck. 2017. "Making Sense of xAPI." *TD at Work.* Alexandria, VA: ATD Press.

References and Resources

Wallace, D. 2021. "Lessons in Learning Design From a Former Marketing and Advertising Pro." Podcast. *Train Like You Listen*, October 12. endurance learning.com/blog/lessons-in-learning-design-from-a-former-marketing -and-advertising-pro.

Wallace, G.W. 2021. *Performance-Based Lesson Mapping and Instructional Development Using a Facilitated Group Process*. Self-published.

Washburn, B. 2022. "Writing Effective Learning Objectives." Podcast. *Train Like You Listen*, January 26. endurancelearning.com/blog/writing-effective -learning-objectives.

Werbach, K., and D. Hunter. 2020. *For the Win: The Power of Gamification and Game Thinking in Business, Education, Government, and Social Impact*. Philadelphia: Wharton School Press.

Index

Page numbers followed by *f* refer to figures.

A

Abode InDesign, 118
accessibility, 11
action items, 80
activities, 34–35. *See also* games
"ADDIE: The Origin of Modern-Day ISD" (Green), 4
ADDIE model of instructional design, xii, 5–20
    actions to take when using, 6*f*
    analyzing as step in, 6–9
    build-borrow-buy matrix for, 159
    designing as step in, 9–12
    developing as step in, 12–13
    evaluating as step in, 13–14
    implementing as step in, 13–14
    as non-linear process, 16, 18
    template for preparing to use, 144–145
Adobe Captivate, 117, 156
Adobe InDesign, 156
Adobe Photoshop, 156
advanced skill building, 25*t*
advertising, 103–104
agenda, for meetings with SMEs, 88
Agile for Instructional Designers (Torrance), xiii
AI (artificial intelligence), 66–68, 67*t*
Allen, Michael, xiii
ambivalent supervisors, 81–82
Analyze step (ADDIE model), 6–9
    in construction company example, 17

skipping over, 39
template for, 144
    in wholesale club example, 15
anchor activities, 35, 38, 39, 116
Anchor-Content-Application-Future Use model, 35–37, 108
Angry Birds (game), 107
animation software, 118, 156
application, in Anchor-Content-Application-Future Use model, 36
application activities, 36, 38, 39, 116
apply content, learners not knowing how to, 80–81
approved vendor lists, 122
art galleries, 101
articles
    in drip campaigns, 65
    follow-up, 80
Articulate (company), 109
Articulate Rise, 117, 156
Articulate Storyline, 117, 156
artificial intelligence (AI), 66–68, 67*t*
Association for Talent Development (ATD), 106, 168
associations, professional, 106
ATD's Handbook for Training and Talent Development, 4
audience(s)
    global, 48
    target, 7–8, 51–52
automation, of drip campaigns, 66
availability, of SMEs, 152

Index

B

barriers to program support, 78–83
  ambivalent/unengaged
    supervisors, 81–82
  anticipating, 8
  forgetting learned content, 79–80
  inability to apply learned content,
    80–81
  lack of access to technology, 81
  opposition by supervisors, 83
  perceived lack of time, 78–79
  reverting to old habits, 79
barriers to transfer of learning, 90–91
Barry, Heather, 88
Beestrum, Molly, 109
behaviors, changing, 10
beta testing, 75–76, 95–96
Beyond the Sky, 103
borrowing resources. *See* outside
  resources
borrowing talent. *See* outside talent
Broad, Mary, 82, 90–92
Brown, Peter C., 65
budgetary constraints, 130–131,
  137–140, 138*f*
budgetary stakeholders, getting buy-in
  from, 72*t*
build-borrow-buy matrix (ADDIE
  model), 137, 138, 159
buy-in, from stakeholders, 70–72, 72*t*

C

campaign, spearheading the
  communication for a new, 63*t*
Canva, 118, 156
Center for Creative Leadership, 61
Certified Eye Bank Technician exam,
  134
champions, finding, 93–95
change, John Kotter's process for
  leading, 70–71
change management, 25*t*
chatbots, 66–68
ChatGPT, 66

cheat sheets, 80
checklists, 80, 82
Clark, Ruth C., 47
closed captioning, 48
coffee, grabbing a, 94–95
Cohen Dan S., 71
colleague(s)
  as beta testers, 95
  covering tasks for a, 64*t*
  as outside resource, 104–105
commercials, 103
committee, representing the team on a
  cross-functional, 64*t*
communities of practice, as outside
  resource, 105–106
competing medium-priority
  compliance training projects
  (worked example), 139, 164–165
completion, determining achievement
  of, 13
compliance training projects,
  competing medium-priority (worked
  example), 139, 164–165
computer systems, 81
construction company (case example),
  17–19
content
  in Anchor-Content-Application-
    Future Use model, 35–36
  evaluating SME's understanding
    of, 152
  identifying sources of, 9
  niche, 131
  outlining, 31, 31*t*–33*t*, 33
contractors, program evaluation, 126
contract workers, supervising, 63*t*
Coursera, 135
covering tasks, for a colleague, 64*t*
COVID-19 pandemic, 59
co-workers, as outside resource,
  104–105
CRAP Test, 109
cross-functional committee,
  representing the team on a, 64*t*
customizing your approach, 141

D

data
    during evaluation phase, 76–77
    to support specific training needs, 7
date and time, of lesson plans, 28
deadlines, 12
debrief, 33t
decision tree, for buying decisions, 114f
Defelice, Robin, 54, 56, 58
delegating a task (stretch assignment), 64t
delivery methods. *See* instructional delivery methods
department managers, 15–16
Design for How People Learn (Dirksen), xiii
Designing Microlearning (Torgerson and Iannone), 58
Design step (ADDIE model), 9–12
    building a team to test the learning program during, 74, 77t
    in construction company example, 17–18
    template for, 144–145
    in wholesale club example, 15–16
Desjardins, Jesse, 117
Develop step (ADDIE model), 12–13
    building a team to test the learning program during, 75, 77t
    in construction company example, 18
    template for, 145
    in wholesale club example, 16
digital learning. *See* e-learning
digital off-the-shelf learning experiences, 134–135
Dirksen, Julie, xiii
diversification of instructional techniques, 37, 37t–38t, 38
doing it yourself, using available tools vs., 114t–115t, 115
dominKnow One, 156

downloads, 80
drip campaigns, 64–66

E

ecosystem, learning. *See* learning ecosystem
editing, 96
ELB Learning, 99
e-learning, 42–45, 46t, 47–48
    advantages of, 42
    in drip campaigns, 65
    involving supervisors before and after, 91t
    off-the shelf content, 130, 134–135
    program objectives, 43–45
    program title, 43
    quality assurance in creating modules for, 75
    storyboard template for, 149
    using an outside vendor to develop, 125
E-Learning and the Science of Instruction (Clark and Mayer), 47
E-Learning Heroes website, 109
Elements of Amazing Learning Experiences, 100f
emails, using AI to provide feedback on, 67t
employee(s)
    leading the search for a new, 63t
    in organizational system, 70
Endurance Learning, 87, 100f, 104
ethical issues, when using outside resources, 100–101
Evaluate step (ADDIE model), 13–14
    building a team to test the learning program during, 76–77, 77t
    in construction company example, 19
    template for, 145
    in wholesale club example, 17
evaluation rubric, 55
executive summaries, in drip campaigns, 65
explainer videos, 60t
eye banks, 73

F

facilitator guides
  creating, 40–42, 41f, 124
  template for, 148
facilitators
  preparation of, 14
  using outside, 126
feedback
  from beta testers, 96
  difficulty of providing, 54–55
  ensuring that you receive
    necessary, 154–155
  from key players, 10
  rubric for, 55
  from SMEs, 89–90
  using AI to provide, 67t
final module review, 155
"5 Key Principles for Designing and
  Delivering Video-Based Learning"
  (Jain), 61
Fiverr, 119
flowcharts, 80
follow-up, post-training, 26t, 80
forgetting, by learners, 79–80
formal learning experience (formal
  training), 21–49
  avoiding PowerPoint in, 21–22
  being ruthless in creating, 22–24
  creating facilitator and participant
    guides for, 40–42, 41f
  e-learning as component of, 42–45,
    46t, 47–48
  estimating time for, 30, 30t, 31, 31t
  importance of intent in creating,
    24, 25t–26t
  instructional delivery methods for,
    33–38, 34t, 37t–38t
  instructor-led training as
    component of, 26–28
  learning objectives in, 28–29
  outlining content and key points
    for, 31, 31t–33t, 33
  reasons not to default to, 51–52
  value of informal training
    compared with, 51–53

*For the Win: The Power of Gamification and
  Game Thinking in Business, Education,
  Government, and Social Impact*
  (Werbach and Hunter), 108
Fortune 500 manufacturing company
  (case example), 3–4
freelance program developers, 125
free trials (software), 115
full-service instructional design, using
  an outside vendor for, 125
future use, in Anchor-Content-
  Application-Future Use model, 36–37

G

game libraries, 107
games, 34, 106–108
gamification, 106
*The Gamification of Learning and
  Instruction: Game-Based Methods and
  Strategies for Training and Education*
  (McGonigal), 108
gaming software, 115–116, 116f, 156
global audiences, 48
goals
  identifying ultimate, 10
  of lesson plans, 27
"good enough," settling for, 38–39
Google, 53, 70, 103, 108, 162
Google Surveys, 156
Google translate, 115t
grammar and spelling, 96
Green, Angel, 4
guides. *See* facilitator guides;
  participant guides

H

handouts, 40–42, 41f, 80
hands-on work, 61
The Heart of Change (Kotter and Cohen),
  71
high-priority projects, balancing
  multiple, 131
Hodell, Chuck, xiii
Houck, Rob, 48

Index

HTML code, using AI to provide, 67t
human body, as system, 70
human connections, building, 73–74
Hunter, Dan, 108

I

Iannone, Sue, 58
ILT. *See* instructor-led training
image files, 48
Implement step (ADDIE model), 13–14
    building a team to test the learning
        program during, 75–76, 77t
    in construction company example,
        18–19
    template for, 145
    in wholesale club example, 16
inclusiveness, 11, 47
individuals, in organizational system,
    70
informal learning experience, 51–68
    AI as component of, 66–68, 67t
    chatbots as component of, 66–68
    drip campaigns as component of,
        64–66
    hands-on work as component of, 61
    job aids as component of, 53,
        53t–54t
    microlearning as component of,
        54–58, 56t–57t
    options to use in creating an, 150
    stretch assignments as component
        of, 61–63, 63t–64t
    value of, compared with formal
        training, 51–53
    videos as component of, 58–61, 60t
initiative, leading the implementation
    of a new, 63t
instructional delivery methods, 33–38,
    34t, 37t–38t, 58
instructional design
    definition of, xv–xvi
    full-service, 125
instructional design models, 4–5, 9. *See
    also* ADDIE model of instructional
    design

instructional design structure, 3–20
    analyzing as step in building, 6–9
    building with, 5–14
    creating, in practice, 14–19
    definition of, 4–5
    designing as step in building, 9–12
    developing as step in building,
        12–13
    evaluating as step in building,
        13–14
    implementing as step in building,
        13–14
    models for, 4–5
instructor-led training (ILT), 26–28
    lesson plan for, 147
    preparing for, 12
intent
    behind using video, 59–60
    knowing your, 24, 25t–26t
internet, as resource, 108–110
interns, supervising, 63t
introduction videos, 60t
ISD from the Ground Up (Hodell), xiii
isEazy, 117, 156

J

Jain, Ajay, 61
job aids, 53, 53t–54t, 65
Jones, Kelly, 9
just-in-time approach, 25t

K

Kahoot, 156
Kapp, Karl M., 54–56, 58, 108
key points, outlining, 31, 31t–33t, 33
Kotter, John P., 70–71, 73

L

languages
    changing e-learning programs to
        other, 48
    translating projects into other,
        74
large language models (LLMs), 66, 67

learners
  getting buy-in from, 72t
  post-training evaluation data from, 76
learning content providers, 135
learning ecosystem, 69–83
  barriers to program support in, 78–83
  and building human connections, 73–74
  and creating a team, 74–77, 77t
  and creating stakeholder buy-in, 70–72, 72t
  and program effectiveness, 69–70
learning experience. *See* formal learning experience; informal learning experience
learning management systems (LMSs), 12, 13, 16, 43, 47, 76, 117, 123, 135
learning needs, 1, 4, 6, 19, 26, 51, 52, 65, 68, 94
learning objectives, 28–29
  of e-learning courses, 43–45
  for microlearning, 58
"Learning Objectives–A Research-Inspired Odyssey" (Thalheimer), 29
Leaving ADDIE for SAM (Allen and Sites), xiii
Lectora, 117, 156
lesson plans
  for instructor-led training, 27–28, 147
  reviewing, 74
  using AI to develop, 67t
LinkedIn, 95, 118, 119
LinkedIn Learning, 135
LLMs (large language models), 66, 67
LMSs. *See* learning management systems
long-form videos, 60t
Louvre, 103
low-lift strategies, to involve supervisors, 93, 153
Lumsden, Jody, 9
lunch conversations, 94

M

Make It Stick: The Science of Successful Learning (Brown et al.), 65
"Making Sense of xAPI" (Torrance and Houck), 48
Marczewski, Andrzej, 99
Margol, Elise Greene, 57–58
marketing, 103–104
materials
  handouts, 40–42, 41f
  in lesson plans, 28
  modifying outside vendors', 123–124
  reviewing, before meeting with SMEs, 88
Mayer, Richard E., 47
McDaniel, Mark A., 65
McGonigal, Jane, 106, 108
medium-priority compliance training projects (worked example), 139, 164–165
meeting(s)
  at Endurance Learning, 104
  planning and facilitating a team, 64t
  with SMEs, 88–89
Mentimeter, 156
metrics
  for completion, 13
  identifying, with help of contractors, 126
  for success, 10–11, 14
microlearning, 54–58, 55, 56t–57t
Microlearning: Short and Sweet (Kapp and Defelice), 54, 58
"Microlearning to Boost the Employee Experience" (Margol), 57–58
Microsoft Excel, using AI to teach, 67t
Microsoft Forms, 156
Microsoft PowerPoint. *See* PowerPoint
Microsoft Word, 124
module review, 155
motivation, 71–72
multiday training across 16 offices within two months (worked example), 140, 166–167
museums, 101–103, 102f

Index

N

name tag switch icebreaker, 32*t*
needs analysis, 57–58, 131
Needs Assessment on a Shoestring (Jones and Lumsden), 9
negotiations, 62
new skill building, 25*t*
Newstrom, John, 82, 90–92
new user onboarding for tech start-up (worked example), 139, 162–163
niche content, 131
no, saying, 22–23

O

objectives. *See* learning objectives
off-the shelf content, 129–135
  deciding whether to use, 130–131
  decision-making survey for using, 158
  definition of, 129–130
  pros and cons of buying, 131, 132*t*–133*t*, 133
  sources of, 134–135
old habits, learners reverting to, 79
Olympics (Winter 1980), xi
on-demand approach, 25*t*
on-the-job performance, transferring training to, 92
opposition, by supervisors, 83
Our Iceberg Is Melting: Changing and Succeeding Under Any Conditions (Kotter and Rathgeber), 71
outline review, 155
outlining content and key points, 31, 31*t*–33*t*, 33
outside resources, 99–110. *See also* outside talent; paying for help
  advertising and marketing, 103–104
  communities of practice, 105–106
  co-workers and colleagues, 104–105
  ethical use of, 100–101
  games, 106–108
  internet, 108–110

museums, 101–103, 102*f*
  profesisonal associations, 106
outside talent, 87–97
  beta testers, 95–96
  champions, 93–95
  pilot groups, 95–96
  SMEs, 87–90
  supervisors, 90–93, 91*t*
outside vendors, 121–128
  creating an effective RFP for, 127
  identifying the right, 122–124
  scorecard for choosing, 157
  situational help from, 125–126

P

participant guides, 13, 40–42, 41*f*, 124
paying for help, 113–135
  animation software, 118
  decision tree for, 114*f*
  off-the shelf solutions, 129–135
  options for, 156
  outside vendors, 121–128
  quiz, gaming, and survey software, 115–116, 116*f*
  rapid authoring tools, 117
  trade-offs of doing it yourself vs., 114*t*–115*t*, 115
  translation services, 118–119
  virtual design software, 117–118
  voice-over services, 119
pensive microlearning, 56*t*
PepsiCo, 103
Performance-Based Lesson Mapping and Instructional Development Using a Facilitated Group Process (Wallace), xiii
performance-based microlearning, 57*t*
periodic table of elements, 99
Periodic Table of Gamification Elements, 99
personnel, involvement of, in program development, 12
perspective, of SMEs, 152
persuasive microlearning, 57*t*
Pierce, Matt, 61

pilot groups, finding, 95–96
pilot programs, 13, 75–76
Pinterest, 109
Pixlr, 156
Play-Doh, 75
podcasts, in drip campaigns, 65
Poll Everywhere, 156
polling, 115–116, 116t
post-instruction microlearning, 56t
post-training follow-up, 26t
PowerPoint (Microsoft PowerPoint), 21–22, 117, 118, 124, 156
PowToon, 156
practice-based microlearning, 57t
preparation microlearning, 56t
prework, 26t
pricing, of off-the-shelf content, 132t, 133t
primary microlearning, 56t
Procter & Gamble, 103
product launches, support 20 new (worked example), 140, 168–169
profesisonal associations, 106
professional collectives, off-the-shelf content from, 134
program support, barriers to. *See* barriers to program support
project sponsors, as champions, 94

Q

quality assurance (QA), 12–13, 75, 124
question of the day, 80
questions, to engage supervisors, 82
quick reference guides, 80
Quizizz, 156
Quizlet, 156
quiz software, 115–116, 116f, 156
quizzes, 80

R

rapid authoring tools, 117, 156
Rathgeber, Holger, 71

Reality Is Broken: Why Games Make Us Better and How They Can Change the World (McGonigal), 106, 108
reference guides, quick, 80
remote learning. *See* e-learning
requests for proposal (RFPs), 127
research reports, in drip campaigns, 65
resistance, anticipating, 8
resources
    borrowing (*See* outside resources)
    providing, to enhance learning, 80
reviewers, 48
RFPs (requests for proposal), 127
Roediger, Henry L., III, 65
rubrics, 80, 82
ruthless, being, 22–24, 146
Ruthless Spectrum, 146

S

scalability, of off-the-shelf content, 132t
SCORM files, 13–14, 155
script review, 155
70-20-10 framework, 61
sharing, by SMEs, 152
shoestring, working on a, xvii–xviii
Sites, Richard, xiii
skill building, 25t
skills, discussing, when meeting with SMEs, 89
skills gap, 52
Skillsoft, 135
SMEs. *See* subject matter experts
Smithsonian Institution, 103
software, 81
    animation, 118, 156
    free versions/trials of, 115
    gaming, 115–116, 116f, 156
    quiz, 115–116, 116f, 156
    survey, 115–116, 116f, 156
    virtual design, 117–118, 156
sources, identifying content, 9
Spacing Learning Events Over Time: What the Research Says (Thalheimer), 65

Index

specialty companies, off-the-shelf content from, 134, 135
specific situations, getting help for, 125–126
spelling and grammar, 96
stakeholders
    creating buy-in from, 70–72, 72t
    delivering presentations to key, 63t
    engagement of, 10
    initial meetings with, 3–4
    turning over final files to, 13
storyboards
    for e-learning (template), 149
    learning objective section of, 45, 46t
    reviewing, 74
    in wholesale club example, 16
strategies for designing instruction, 4.
    See also instructional design models
stretch assignments, 61–63, 63t–64t
structure. *See* instructional design structure
subject matter experts (SMEs)
    as champions, 94
    qualification sheet for (template), 152
    testing of the learning program by, 74
    value of, 121
    working with, 87–90
success
    determining, with outside vendors, 124
    increasing the potential for (worksheet), 151
    metrics for determining, 10–11, 14
supervisors
    active opposition by, 83
    ambivalent or unengaged, 81–82
    and decision to forgo formal training, 52
    getting buy-in from, 72t
    low-lift strategies to involve, 93, 153
    post-training evaluation data from, 76
    working with, 90–93, 91t

support 20 new product launches over the next year (worked example), 140, 168–169
SurveyMonkey, 156
survey software, 115–116, 116f, 156
systems thinking, 69–70

T

talent, borrowing. *See* outside talent
target audience
    asking about the, 7–8
    and decision to forgo formal training, 51–52
    finding beta testers from your, 95
    supervisors blocking access to, 83
task force, organizing a, 63t
tasks
    covering, for a colleague, 64t
    delegating, 64t
TD at Work, 48, 57–58
team, building, to test the learning program, 74–77, 77t
team meeting, planning and facilitating a, 64t
team members, leading the search for new, 63t
technical services, companies specializing in, 109
technology(-ies)
    learners not having access to, 81
    vendors' experience with, 123
tech start-up, new user onboarding for (worked example), 139, 162–163
terminology, reviewing, 96
Thalheimer, Will, 29, 65
time
    estimating, 30, 30t, 31, 31t
    learners' perceived lack of, 78–79
    spacing repetitions over, 65
time constraints, 8, 139, 139f, 140
Tire Industry Association, 134
titles
    of e-learning courses, 43
    of lesson plans, 27

Torgerson, Carla, 58
Torrance, Megan, xiii, 48
trade associations, off-the-shelf content from, 134
trainers, using outside, 126
training ambassadors, SMEs as, 152
training company websites, 109
train-the-trainer programs, 14, 16
transfer of learning, barriers to, 90–91
Transfer of Training: Action-Packed Strategies to Ensure High Payoff From Training Investment (Broad and Newstrom), 82, 92
translation services, 115t, 118–119
trust, maintaining, 21
tutorials, 55
TV commercials, 103

U

Udemy, 135
ultimate outcome, identifying, 10
unengaged supervisors, 81–82
updates, to off-the-shelf content, 132t
urgency, of learning needs, 131

V

vendors. *See* outside vendors
verbatim scripts, avoiding, 40
vetted vendor lists, 122
videos, 58–61, 60t
    in drip campaigns, 65
    as follow-up item, 80
video tutorials, 60t
virtual design software, 117–118, 156
virtual museum tours, 103
voice-overs, 45, 46t, 47, 115t
voice-over services, 119
Vyond, 156

W

Wallace, Danielle, 103
Wallace, Guy W., xiii

Washburn, Brian, 29
Web Content Accessibility Guidelines (WCAG), 11
websites, training company, 109
"We need training" (examples), 15–19
Werbach, Kevin, 108
Wescott, Lauren, 96, 155
What's Your Formula? Combine Learning Elements for Impactful Training (Washburn), 99
wholesale club (case example), 3–4, 15–17
Winter Olympics (1980), xi
worked example scenarios
    competing medium-priority compliance training projects, 139, 164–165
    multiday training across 16 offices within two months, 140, 166–167
    new user onboarding for tech start-up, 139, 162–163
    support 20 new product launches over the next year, 140, 168–169
"Writing Effective Learning Objectives" (Washburn), 29

X

xAPI (Experience Application Programming Interface), 48

Y

"Your Year for Video! Getting Started, Leveling Up, and Making Better Videos" (Pierce), 61
"You Suck at PowerPoint" (virtual slide deck), 117
YouTube, 53, 55, 80, 109

Z

Zoom, 59

About the Author

 Brian Washburn is the co-founder and CEO of Endurance Learning, a small, fun, and friendly instructional design firm specializing in generating creative and unique instructor-led or e-learning programs for a client base that ranges from small nonprofit organizations to Fortune 500 companies.

Brian has been dabbling in the world of instructional design and corporate training for more than 25 years. It all began as a Peace Corps volunteer in Paraguay (1998–2000) where he discovered the joys of standing in front of a group of participants, finding ways to engage them, and using flipchart to generate dynamic visual aids.

Since then, Brian has worked mostly in the nonprofit sector, leading training teams that have been charged with world-changing missions ranging from ensuring every child in foster care has a safe and permanent home to eliminating corneal blindness around the globe. Brian has developed and facilitated training programs in North America, South America, Europe, Asia, and Africa. Years ago, he was named a "Top Young Trainer" by *Training* magazine, and more recently, he served as the president of the ATD Puget Sound chapter, ushering it through the COVID-19 pandemic. His first book, *What's Your Formula? Combine Learning Elements for Impactful Training*, was published by ATD Press in 2021.

Brian holds a master's in organization development. He is always happy to connect with people on LinkedIn or to grab virtual coffee and talk all things training and development. He lives in Seattle, Washington, with his wife, two children, and a dog named Picco.

About ATD

atd The Association for Talent Development (ATD) is the world's largest association dedicated to those who develop talent in organizations. Serving a global community of members, customers, and international business partners in more than 100 countries, ATD champions the importance of learning and training by setting standards for the talent development profession.

Our customers and members work in public and private organizations in every industry sector. Since ATD was founded in 1943, the talent development field has expanded significantly to meet the needs of global businesses and emerging industries. Through the Talent Development Capability Model, education courses, certifications and credentials, memberships, industry-leading events, research, and publications, we help talent development professionals build their personal, professional, and organizational capabilities to meet new business demands with maximum impact and effectiveness.

One of the cornerstones of ATD's intellectual foundation, ATD Press offers insightful and practical information on talent development, training, and professional growth. ATD Press publications are written by industry thought leaders and offer anyone who works with adult learners the best practices, academic theory, and guidance necessary to move the profession forward.

We invite you to join our community. Learn more at td.org.